rooms to grow in

Susan Salzman

rooms to grow in

Little Folk Art's great rooms for babies, kids, and teens

susan salzman **and** daryn eller

photography by art streiber

Clarkson Potter/Publishers
New York

Published by Clarkson Potter/Publishers, New York, New York.
Member of the Crown Publishing Group.

Random House, Inc. New York, Toronto, London, Sydney, Auckland
www.randomhouse.com

Clarkson N. Potter is a trademark and Potter and colophon are registered
trademarks of Random House, Inc.

Printed in China

DESIGN BY JANE TREUHAFT

Library of Congress Cataloging-in-Publication Data
is available upon request.

ISBN 0-609-60709-X

10   9   8   7   6   5   4   3   2   1

First Edition

for

grandma rose,

whom I've missed every day for the past eleven

years and who taught me to appreciate cooking,

the home, family, and unconditional love

contents

introduction

Nestled in my son Eli's room are the same Raggedy Ann and Andy dolls that inhabited my bedroom when I was a child. Eli is now also the proud owner of the blocks my brother bought for me on my first birthday and heir to the pint-size rocking chair I rocked in when I, too, was pint-size. We even have the grown-up-size rocking chair in which my mother used to lull us children off to sleep. And I wouldn't part with them for the world.

Of course, there are many items from my childhood room that I'm glad have been relegated to garage-sale heaven. I don't, for instance, bemoan the loss of the yellow shag carpeting that covered my floor or the oh-so-seventies Formica bedroom set with lemon-and-lime trim. Still, when those items were new, I thought they were the living end, and I adored the idea that they were nobody else's but mine.

One of the loveliest and most loving gifts you can give a child is a room that makes him feel special. It might be a big room or a small room, a room that is shared or a room of his own. It might be a hideaway adorned with family heirlooms or a chamber appointed with brand-new furnishings—all that is incidental. What matters is that the room be a warm, safe place that nurtures your child's daydreams during waking hours and brings him sweet dreams at night.

It should be a sanctuary both fanciful and functional, created with an eye toward fostering a child's play, but not at the expense of his parents' sanity—or their sense of style.

There's no better way to produce a homey, comforting environment for a child than to fill it with items, both old

left: Some toys are better off displayed than played with. These vintage stuffed dolls and animals are shown off in a hanging cabinet with chicken-wire doors. opposite: Proof that simple can be sumptuous: The beauty of this handcrafted plane lies in its elegantly elementary workmanship.

and new, that were crafted with loving care from fine materials. They need not necessarily have been created with a child's use in mind. Consider furnishings like time-worn dressers with carved reliefs and glass knobs; weathered picnic tables; wooden beds hand-painted with floral motifs; faded hooked rugs; or wicker baskets and wooden crates in mellow colors. Modern materials such as plastic, pressed wood, and Formica certainly have their place, but it's possible to design practical rooms without the glare of synthetics—rooms that, instead, hark back to simpler times.

When I decided to call my company Little Folk Art, I did so with the idea that folk art—homespun-style objects and furnishings that have a straightforward, heartfelt beauty—bridges the generational gap between parents and children perfectly. Kids are drawn to the whimsy of these pieces, while adults appreciate their nostalgic quality. What's more, furnishings that have had a prior life (or are made to look like they have) are virtually kid-proof. You don't have to worry about a child putting his mud-encrusted shoes up on a table when someone else's shoes have already been on it a thousand times.

Distinctive fabrics also go a long way toward creating rooms that both parents and children can love. Fabrics warm up a room and give a room personality. Pillows with a vintage sports motif, for instance, set the tone for a Little Leaguer's room just as pink taffeta curtains lend a sense of girlish charm to the quarters of a budding teen. A chair upholstered in kaleidoscopic quilts and chenille contributes to the happy mood of a playroom, and a witty mix of plaids staves off formality in an otherwise traditional family room.

But folk-art furnishings and gorgeous fabrics are not all it takes to create rooms to meet your family's requirements. Bedrooms, playrooms, family rooms, even bathrooms need to evolve as children grow, but they shouldn't necessitate a major overhaul every few years. And they won't—provided you employ a key element of smart design: foresight.

As any parent knows, kids grow up way too fast. Before you turn around, an infant's crib has given way to a big-girl's bed, a toddler's pile of stuffed animals to a seven-year-old's collection of skateboards. In fact, children go through so many stages from birth through their teens that you could conceivably make over their rooms every two years (if not more often). So as ludicrous as it may seem to worry about where a computer is going to go before a baby is even born, it pays to look at a room with an eye to the future. And when I say it pays, I mean that literally. Using a little foresight to ensure that a child's room needs only minor tinkering to keep up with its rapidly maturing occupant will save you money—and cut down on the stress of having to rethink a room repeatedly. Ideally, you'll decorate a room and be done with it for several years.

This book aims to help you think about various environments in both the present and the future tense. My goal is also to help you solve problems. Just about every kind of room presents its own particular challenge. It might be size, awkward architecture (what were they thinking?), or lack of wall space. Shared rooms always present unique challenges, as do rooms that need to house specific collections or accommodate a child's particular interests. Trying to achieve a certain style—say, Country French or Americana—while keeping the rooms child-friendly can also be a challenge. And just about every child's room has a storage problem.

Let's be frank: most kids have a lot of stuff. Let this stuff get out of control and it will swallow up their bedrooms—and possibly the rest of the house, too. While you can certainly throw everything into a couple of plastic bins and a big toy box, there are far more inventive—and far more attractive—ways to attack the storage problem. That's why throughout these pages, you'll find tons of ideas for keeping your kids' stuff organized without compromising the aesthetic appeal of your home.

This whole book, in fact, is about ideas, some that you may want to duplicate to a T, others that you may want to adapt to suit your own home. My aim is to get you thinking about new resources for decorating and help you learn to hunt for furnishings with a sharper eye. Ultimately, I hope you will take elements of Little Folk Art style and create a look that's uniquely your own.

Environmentalist Rachel Carson once wrote, "If a child is to keep alive his inborn sense of wonder, he needs the companionship of at least one adult who can share it, rediscovering with him the joy, excitement, and mystery of the world we live in." And what better place to begin cultivating a child's sense of wonder than in a home designed with imagination and love.

Expect the unexpected: Atop this colonial-style bed, South American fabrics are combined with a patchwork of all-American plaids. Instead of the usual painting or poster, an old toy airplane decorates the wall above this young boy's bed.

1 getting started

Parents often give more time and attention to the rooms their children occupy than they do to their own rooms. But that's not so surprising. We want only the best for our children, and that includes rooms that are well appointed for sleep, play, and learning. We want spaces that will feel uniquely personal and that our kids can feel proud of. In the case of new babies, we also want—let's admit it—the perfect place to showcase our pride and joy.

Creating rooms for children isn't all that different from creating rooms for adults, but there are some important distinctions. Kids can easily outgrow a room if it isn't plotted wisely, and their rooms are usually little worlds unto themselves, places that must accommodate sleep, play, learning, socializing, and family hours. Sometimes kids' rooms need to keep more than one child happy, leaving the designer (you) faced with the tricky task of striking an acceptable balance. And storage is an issue in virtually every child's space I design.

design basics

I'm not a big believer in design rules. If something works, it works, even if it goes against what might be considered design gospel. Yet, that said, there are a few basics that will help get you started and keep you from making errors you'll regret later.

consider your budget

When you're redoing your child's room, it's easy to make do with what you have, replacing furnishings one by one as needed and as your budget allows. It's harder, of course, if you have a newborn on the way and are starting from scratch. But keep in mind that you needn't have every last detail in place when you bring your baby home from the hospital. New babies actually need very little (see Nursery Essentials, page 22).

Whether you have $500 or $5,000 to spend, you want your money to go as far as possible. To do that, you need a plan so that you don't end up spending haphazardly and less wisely than you should. First, make a wish list: *"If I could get everything I wanted, this is what I'd get . . ."* Then, prioritize: *"I must have a crib, so the toile curtains will have to wait . . ."* Or see what compromises you can make: *"I'll buy a second-hand crib from a consignment shop so I can also buy the toile curtains . . ."* Last, set a goal: *"In twelve months, I want everything to be complete."*

Once you've covered these very basic considerations, you're ready to start in on the fun part: the design.

think about function

Think long and hard about how your child's room will actually be used, both now and down the line. Will there be a computer in the room, or is there a place for study in another part of the house? How much play will go on here? Do you need a place for sleep-over guests? A table for model building or a trunk to hold dress-up clothes? Your aim should be to create a room that's not only pleasing to your eye, but also practical.

pick a design focus

The most common question people ask me about designing children's rooms is "Where should I start?" There's no single answer to that query, but I have a suggestion that can help: Zero in on one element of the room and let that be your guide. That one element can be anything. It might be a particular fabric. It might be a certain style, such as country cottage or fifties kitsch. It might be a wonderful piece of furniture.

If, for instance, you fall in love with a sleigh bed, use that to launch your design plan. A wicker crib, for instance, may lead you to choose wallpaper and accessories that echo its gardeny feel. If your child has a collection of musical instruments, vintage movie posters, or ballet paraphernalia, you may want to build the room around pieces that will best exhibit her collectibles. Perhaps you're enamored of the Shaker look. Focus your search, then, on furnishings in keeping with that aesthetic, then add some cozy rugs and playful wall hangings to soften up the overall look. As long as you have *something* to set the tone for a room, it doesn't really matter what drives your inspiration.

bring your child into the process

Nurseries, unquestionably, reflect the tastes of moms and dads; after all, you can't be expected to incorporate your baby's style into the room when he hasn't even formed one yet. But as your child starts developing a personality, as well as

likes and dislikes, you'll want that personality to resonate throughout the environment. For instance, when I was initially putting together my son's room, I displayed some of the stuffed animals and dolls that I had been purchasing at flea markets for many years. But as he grew, he became fascinated with vehicles and trucks in particular. (I venture to say that I now know more about front loaders and tractors than most construction workers.) It was then that I began showcasing a collection of antique trucks on the shelves in his room.

Once your child is old enough to speak his mind,

Consider being a collector on your young child's behalf. At first haunting flea markets for vintage toy trucks was my passion; now my son enjoys the hunt, too.

ask what kinds of furnishings and colors he'd like in his room—and be prepared to listen to his answer. When the young son in one family I was working with was asked what color bed he wanted, he chose orange. His mother's heart sank and so did mine; we both knew that that orange bed wasn't going to stand the test of time. It turned out that the boy also loved purple, so we managed to warm him up to the idea of having some orange accents in the room and going with a deep-grape-colored bed instead. The trick, I think, was not reacting (visibly) with disdain to his ideas, but rather guiding him toward more palatable (and ultimately more practical) choices. When the room was done, he loved it and, having had some input, felt proud of it, too. And he still sleeps in the grape-colored bed today.

a place for everything

The first few years of parenthood are filled with revelations about all kinds of things. One of them is that, when you have kids, there is no such thing as too much storage space. Children's possessions multiply at an alarming rate and it doesn't take long for toys and things to begin overwhelming the house. Suddenly, no room is safe from clutter and disarray.

Solving storage dilemmas comes down to one word: organization. You might even say micro-organization. I am famous for putting storage units within storage units—baskets, say, within a bookshelf or wire boxes in a closet—because it makes it that much easier to keep things from becoming messy and jumbled. The more contained your family's belongings are, the easier it will be for both you and your children to find them and use them as they were intended.

As long, that is, as what you're storing is also accessible. A stack of games won't get played if no one can reach them. Clothes will go unworn if they're in boxes with tight-fitting lids that a five-year-old can't open.

Ample and well-designed cabinets and closets are the ideal solution to all storage problems, but if you don't have them, there are other options. It's possible to find many attractive storage vessels that actually add to the look of a room, and sometimes these vessels—the oddly shaped basket, the garage-sale rack—can be fitted into places in the house that might otherwise just be wasted space. Don't overlook anything that can be pressed into service.

left: An oversize basket hung on the wall doubles as a toy box. A basket like this can also work as a clothes hamper. above: Designate a vessel for each type of toy. Here, separate containers hold balls, books, Frisbees, and protective helmets.

put those toys away, please

When you go about ordering your children's toys, it helps to think about them just as you would the staples in a business office (toys, after all, are your children's "work"). That is, have a different container for every category of object. You might, for instance, place all the balls in one container; transportation items (i.e., trucks, cars, trains) in another; and musical instruments in yet another. Have separate containers for dolls and doll clothes.

The containers can be anything you like: wicker baskets, wire baskets, galvanized buckets, garden receptacles, hatboxes, wooden crates from the wine store. I also like cardboard file boxes—some stores sell variations on the theme that are quite elegant looking—since they're lightweight and are easy for children to maneuver.

above: Found objects can net you a lot of extra storage space. This one, intended for fishermen's use, was obtained at a flea market, but marine supply shops have similar items. below: For superheroes who need to make a quick escape, hooks make clothes and other items easy to grab—and put away. opposite: Painted symbols on crates help children who can't yet read learn where things go.

If, however, a container isn't already good-looking, you can make it more decorative. Paint baskets to complement the colors of your child's room, or cover wooden and cardboard boxes with adhesive paper or vintage wallpaper. It's a good idea, too, to label each vessel with words or pictures so that your child will know where to find what—and where everything goes when it's cleanup time. In my home I have a set of nine crates, all painted the same color and each labeled with a different toy category. These crates have helped my son become a good cleaner-upper. Today, if you mistakenly put an animal in the truck box, he'll be the first to let you know!

Once you have a good collection of containers, think about keeping them organized on shelves, in cabinets, and in closets. If you already own a big toy box, consider putting smaller boxes (for Lego, for instance) inside to avoid a big muddle of toys.

clothes-minded

If you are lucky enough to have a large closet, you probably won't have much trouble storing your child's clothes. But even a small closet may offer more storage space than you realize. Think about the different ways you can configure the space and add "helpers" like shoe racks and soft hanging shelves made from fabric.

You will notice as you go through this book that I'm a great fan of armoires. You can buy them—or have old ones revamped—with a combination of hanging space and shelves. Dressers, of course, are a logical option as well, although you may want to consider customizing your child's dresser. I often put dividers in the drawers, which make it easier for kids to keep the stacks of folded clothes neat. Dividers can also be used in drawers to separate toys like dolls from other playthings like puzzles and games.

Hooks and knobs are a great help when it comes to keeping your child's clothes neat and accessible. Outfitting your child's closet with hooks that are within his arm's reach will give him a place to hang packs, hats, and jackets. Peg racks and clothes trees all help prevent clothes from piling up on the floor, too, as will placing a hamper in the room.

reclaim wasted space

Many rooms have strange architectural oddities or alcoves created by furniture that, most times, go to waste. Put this space to use by either filling it with storage vessels or outfitting it with shelves. In alcoves where shelves aren't appropriate, but floor space is available, place boxes or baskets. Choose those with lids so they can be stacked. And don't forget about the space under beds and cribs. Children's toys can be placed in boxes or crates and stored under their beds. Under cribs, you may want to store blankets and linens that you don't use on a daily basis or gifts that your child won't be using for a while.

If you have storage on the brain, you'll be surprised at how many ideas you'll come up with. Suddenly, things that seemed useless before will reveal themselves to be the perfect container for marbles or a great place for stashing dirty clothes.

2 oh, baby!

When faced with the task of creating a nursery, far too many parents fall prey to the belief that they must buy absolutely everything ever made to ensure their infant's comfort. But before you go out and spend a fortune (or feel bad because you don't have a fortune to spend), recognize that in reality you don't need all that much. You'll certainly want to design a beautiful room for that little bundle (or bundles) of joy, but you can accomplish this goal simply—and without bankrupting the college fund.

On the following pages, you'll find a checklist to help you out as well as four nurseries that range from frugal to lavish in style.

nursery essentials

crib It's tempting to blow most of your money on a crib, but you might want to temper that urge. The time an infant spends in a crib is relatively brief—usually no more than three years—and it ultimately ends up in an attic or passed on to a friend. The most important thing is to buy a crib that's *safe*. Whether you purchase a new one or employ a hand-me-down, make sure it meets these safety recommendations from the U.S. Consumer Product Safety Commission:

- Check for missing, loose, broken, or improperly installed screws, brackets, or other hardware on the crib or mattress support.
- There should be no more than $2\frac{3}{8}$ inches between crib slats; anything wider may allow the baby's body to slip through.
- Be certain the mattress is firm and snug-fitting so the baby cannot get trapped between it and the side of the crib. (Also consider buying a hypoallergenic mattress.)
- Corner posts must not be more than $\frac{1}{16}$ inch higher than the end panels (unless they are over 16 inches high for a canopy). The baby's clothing may catch on a higher post and strangle him or her.
- The crib must not have any cutout areas on the head or footboard; these could cause the baby's head to get trapped.
- The crib's mattress support should not easily pull away from the corner posts. Otherwise the baby could get trapped between mattress and crib.

If the crib passes these tests you'll also want to do the following:

- Repair any cracked or peeling paint to prevent lead poisoning.
- Check for splinters or rough edges.

changing table/dresser Although changing tables are nice, unless they're very aesthetically appealing or function to perfection, you might be better off spending your money on a great dresser that will have a long life and putting a pad for changing on top. You can have a top made for it if you feel a pad isn't enough, but the economical solution is to just have a custom pad made and covered

Removable tops are easy to add. This one helped turn a $100 thrift shop find into a great changing table.

with a great fabric. People often ask me, "Won't the baby fall off?" or "Doesn't the top need a lip?" The answer is no. As long as you're there guarding your baby, he won't fall off (and an infant should never be left unattended on a changing table at any rate, no matter how it's configured). Once your child no longer needs the changing pad, you can just remove it. You're left with a useful and practical dresser that can stay in the family for years.

One last word about dressers: Some of them have cabinet fronts, which hide drawers and open out. They are great looking but ultimately not great for children. When kids reach the age of three or so, they like to start dressing themselves. Having at least some exposed drawers that they can access will help give them a sense of independence.

rocking chair Rockers are especially wonderful during the first year of a child's life, before she gets too mobile and has the desire to wander and explore. And there are so many great rockers to choose among, from wooden and upholstered styles to glider and vintage versions. Think about purchasing a rocker that will fit in somewhere else in the house when you're ready to remove it from your child's room. Wooden rockers are particularly adaptable, though my favorites are upholstered rockers (like the one on page 84). They can be slipcovered in cotton for the summer and in a heavier fabric for the winter months. Slipcovers are also easy to wash should your baby have an accident. Consider getting a footstool or ottoman to go with your rocker; your tired feet will probably need the rest.

lamp Overhead lights are fine, but many children like to fall asleep with the light on, in which case a table lamp with a three-way bulb comes in handy. You can put it on at 25 watts for lullaby time, 75 watts when you want to read or play. Think twice, though, about buying a babyish lamp—it may seem too infantile after a year or so.

shelves You're bound to receive a lot of lovely gifts such as silver cups and rattles for your child, and you'll need someplace to display them. There will, though, be some things you want your child to have access to and some things you don't. Whether you choose mounted wall shelves or standing bookshelves, keep your child's stuff low and the items for "show," such as collections and keepsakes, high. In my son's room, I placed a low bookshelf under the window so that he can choose the things he wants to play with, but I kept some things like antique trucks and a collection of fragile Steiff stuffed animals out of reach.

bedding Initially you'll just want a sheet for the crib and a blanket or two, since soft, bulky items such as pillows or comforters are dangerous: they can cause suffocation. As your child gets older, you may want to buy quilts or purchase fabric and have something made up. You can even take an old quilt or blanket that you have loved over the years and make it into something special for your baby.

pictures Whether it's art or family photographs, give your baby something beautiful to look at.

stocking up:
more goodies for the good of your child
(and a few to skip)

Natural baby toiletries

Cloth diapers for spit ups, burping, and 101 other uses

Cloth or disposable diapers

Diaper covers

Hooded towels

Wipes or water and cloth for cleanup

forget

Diaper Genie

Baby swing

Bouncy seat

Crib vibrator

Wipe warmers

waste basket Not to be confused with a diaper pail (see below). Because I have a dog that gets into things, I opted for a small wooden trash can with a lid. I line it with a plastic bag, then take out the trash as needed.

set of bumpers Padded bumpers keep the baby from rolling into the slats. Here again, you can buy premade sets or choose your own fabric and have some made for you.

waterproof mattress cover Trust me, you'll find out soon enough how useful this is. Don't make up the crib without it!

optional furnishings

rug If you don't have carpeting (or if you do and want to hide it), a throw rug will help warm up the room. The options are endless and will depend on the décor you've chosen.

diaper pail I say optional because I've never loved the idea of accumulating dirty diapers in a child's room. I always take used diapers out of the room and throw them in the big trash can. However, if you're using cloth or don't want to make the trip to the can each time, a diaper pail is a worthy investment. Look for one that you may be able to reuse later as a hamper or storage unit.

hamper A hamper is certainly convenient, but if you're short on space, consider it optional. I prefer to take all dirty items out of the room as they're cast off and toss them into the central laundry area.

dust ruffle I like the look of a crib with a dust ruffle, and it provides another opportunity to add some color and pattern to the room. A dust ruffle also allows you to store toys and other items under the crib, and no one's the wiser.

receiving blankets Chances are you'll be given several as gifts, so don't bother buying them until you know for sure you'll need them.

double the fun

In some cases I agree with Mies van der Rohe's famous pronouncement that less is more. On the other hand, sometimes more really *is* more—it looks just great. But what is it that makes some rooms that are chock-full of furnishings and collectibles work while others look like pandemonium has broken loose?

There is nothing moderate about this nursery, including the fact that it belongs to lively twenty-two-month-old twin boys, Ethan and Noah. The mere fact that it is home to twins ensures that a room will have more of almost everything, although in the early years when many of their belongings are still small, a single dresser and closet provide adequate clothing storage for two.

Here, that left plenty of space for the boys' parents to display a vast collection of Americana. Over the years they had assembled an array of items, ranging from flag art and wobble-head dolls to toy sailboats and old tops. Knowing that they wanted to show off the collectibles in the twins' nursery, I worked with them to design a room that would complement the all-Americana theme.

Choosing the colors was easy. Red, white,

Framed reprints from children's readers are displayed above the cribs. The narrow wicker and wood bookcases, home to collectibles and small storage boxes, were picked up dirt cheap at a garage sale. Originally bright yellow, they were painted a brick red.

and blue was the obvious choice—and a necessary one if we wanted all that paraphernalia to blend in harmoniously. Much of what makes this room work despite its vast number of elements is that the colors were kept within a narrow range. Going with a less patriotic palette might have been a bit too much for the eye to take in.

Selecting fabrics with simple patterns—plaids and stripes—also helped keep chaos at bay and allowed for one bold exception: A rug with a red, white, and blue phoenix motif that complements the room's nostalgic feel.

As Ethan and Noah have grown, their room has evolved slightly. A rocking chair for Mom has been replaced by a club chair and ottoman for the boys that's covered in a nubby white chenille and blue and white plaid. Flea-market finds that used to cover one of the nursery's walls were removed to make way for an art board that's outfitted perfectly for twins: While one scribbles on the chalkboard, the other can draw on paper pulled from the other side.

Caring for twins, as the boys' parents will readily attest, can be trying at times, but it can be a much easier job if you keep a sense of humor. To that end, Ethan and Noah's room was designed to be whimsical and light, setting the stage for hours of family fun.

opposite, top: Crates similar in size and shape to shirt boxes keep the changing table's shelves neat. Hung above and to the right of the table are pull toys cleverly framed so you can still give the strings a tug. On a bamboo side table, a lamp sheds light on books and toys. Its base is an old oil can. opposite, bottom: Crib sheets don't have to be white or even light. Here, deep blue flannel gives the crib a cozy feel. right: Vintage wobble-head baseball players, a worn ball, and a child's wall hanging share space with the twins' toiletries.

above: For display and play: gently worn tops and painted metal baseball memorabilia. right: It's never too soon to get kids to appreciate the great American pastime. Here, a treasure trove of old baseballs stack up in a wire basket painted red. opposite: The windows in this room were covered with inexpensive paper shades from an import store that complement the wood floors and doors. Setting them off is an easy fix: Yards of striped cotton ticking were simply wrapped around a curtain rod and hemmed at the bottom to prevent fraying.

creating a safe haven

The final weeks before a baby is born are usually the most harried. Fresh paint goes on the walls, new carpet is laid, just-bought furniture is installed. But the by-products of all this newness—chemicals—can be harmful to babies' developing brains and organs, particularly since, pound for pound, infants breathe in more air than adults do, making them especially vulnerable to toxins. So before you bring children of any age into redecorated rooms, take the following precautions:

- Most paints, wallpaper adhesives, and varnishes sold these days are safe for children if they are given adequate time to "off gas"—that is, to release hazardous chemicals, many of which help them dry. Optimally, newly painted and wallpapered rooms should be given four to eight weeks of open-window ventilation to air out. Give new furniture and mattresses time to air out, too.

- Use your nose. If you can smell chemicals, they probably haven't dissipated yet.

- Chemical dissipation is particularly crucial when it comes to carpet. While seemingly innocuous, new carpet is the source of many complaints received by the Consumer Products Safety Commission (CPSC) and can cause everything from runny noses to headaches, rashes, and fatigue. The CPSC advises leaving the house the day carpeting is installed, then opening the windows and running fans *and* air conditioning for three days to maximize ventilation.

- Consider forgoing carpet and using untreated cotton or wool throw rugs, which can be shaken out often and cleaned easily. Rugs are also less likely to trap molds and fungus.

- When buying anything for a new baby's room, carpet to changing tables, ask about environmentally friendly options. Some stores, for instance, sell paints with low VOC (volatile organic compounds). Furniture that is either unpainted or made of hardwood rather than pressed wood (which is usually treated with chemicals) is also worth considering for these reasons.

- If you're pregnant, don't do any painting or stripping yourself, especially if your house was built before 1978, since it may still have lead paint. Lead and VOCs can cross the placenta.

unexpected pleasures

There are many things that we associate instantly
with nurseries. Mobiles. Storybook art. Decorative borders on the wall. There
are just as many things we'd never associate with nurseries, yet they can work
very well to make a baby's room beautiful and unique.

In the nursery I created for Lionel and Diane Richie's daughter Sofia, much
of the eye appeal comes from objects collected by her mother from flea markets

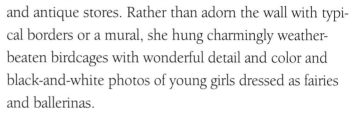

and antique stores. Rather than adorn the wall with typical borders or a mural, she hung charmingly weather-
beaten birdcages with wonderful detail and color and
black-and-white photos of young girls dressed as fairies
and ballerinas.

While not everything an adult collects will look
appropriate in a child's nursery, you may already have a
collection at hand that will work in your baby's room. Or
you may want to use the occasion of her birth to start a
collection. If so, think about directing your hunt toward
the practical. Here, along with the black-and-white photos and birdcages, a collection of fishermen's baskets and
a jumbo fishing net not only contribute to the room's
great eclectic look, they add to its storage capabilities,
too. Antiques can function the same way.

Another element responsible for this room's distinctive style is the play of dark wood against white walls and
white accents like the chenille chair, bumpers, and changing pad. Aside from
the color of Sofia's toys and a few of the room's accoutrements, the nursery is
very neutral—but it nonetheless looks warm and inviting. Originally, the crib,
changing table, and stool resided in Sofia's brother Miles's room. In those days,
they were painted red, white, and blue. Diane wanted a different look for Sofia,
so we stripped the pieces, then stained them a rich walnut shade and changed
the hardware to crystal doorknobs (another unexpected touch). It's a perfect

opposite: Found objects—an old birdcage, wire and picnic baskets, and a fishing net—add to
this nursery's uncommon beauty. above: In an understated room, an arrangement of leather
masks and a bamboo peg rack provides some drama.

example of why it pays to recycle: You can get a whole new look for a fraction of the cost.

Much has been made of the idea that a room must have bright colors in order to engage a baby, but I disagree. Here, offbeat objects work just as well to captivate a curious child, and sticking to subtle tones gives the nursery an aura of calm.

above: A picnic basket lined with an old remnant of chenille makes a perfect home for dolls and books. left: Each of these shelves is different from the others. Scattering them along the wall rather than hanging them in a traditional fashion highlights their individuality. Replacing classic hardware with crystal doorknobs makes for high impact against the grain of the changing table's dark wood. below: Bringing the outside in: Clay garden pots nestled into a wire bottle holder make great receptacles for cotton swabs, cotton balls, hair accessories, and other little-girl items.

opposite: The ballerina collectibles were assembled by Sofia's mother, a dancer herself. While most ballet-themed collectibles are cutesy, these are sophisticated and won't seem babyish as Sofia grows.

nursery on a budget

After the excitement of discovering you're pregnant
dies down, your thoughts will inevitably turn to practical things. Naturally,
chief among them will be what to do to your baby's room. That is, assuming you *have* a room for the baby. Plenty of couples start out by converting a
closet into a tiny space for their newborn or even keeping the baby in their
own room for as long as possible.

Depending on a couple's financial situation, outfitting the baby's room
can be a joy or a source of stress. Yet even if you don't have a lot to spend
on a nursery, don't let it spoil even one minute of this glorious time. Trust
me: A little money can still go a long way.

When I met one young couple who wanted to create a nursery on a
budget, the wife was five months pregnant. At the time, all they knew was
that they were having a little girl and that their financial resources were limited to $2,500. That's not at all a bad sum, but even if you have less to work
with you can learn from some of their wise decisions.

For starters, the couple determined that they would buy one big-ticket
item and scrimp on the rest. The luxury piece they chose was a custom-
made armoire—a necessity because the husband has appropriated the
closet in the baby's room. Older homes and apartments are often short on
closets and an armoire is the perfect antidote. If you can't afford a new one,
buy a secondhand armoire, then have the interior redone to include both
shelves and rods. That way you can fill it with hanging clothes, folded items,
and shoes. A redo only costs a couple hundred dollars and, added to the
price of a flea-market find, will total far less than a new piece.

Several of the other furnishings in the nursery were antique-shop finds.
The dresser/changing table was purchased for $100, then stripped and
repainted (see the original on page 42). We also changed the hardware,
replaced the architectural molding, and planed the runners so the drawers
pulled out smoothly. Because the dresser was a little low, we put wheels

**Think overhead and underneath for your storage needs. Here, a shelf was hung over the
changing table, while a crate was slipped underneath to add more "drawer" space.**

on it to give it some height—important since nothing can give you a bad back quicker than having to bend over to change a baby several times a day. Finally, a changing top with pad was added. Eventually, it will be removed and the piece will revert back to being a simple dresser.

Another antique purchase was the crib. Old wooden cribs can be much more special and unique than newer ones, many of which are made of pressboard. Buying an old crib can be a bit dicey, though, since some of them don't conform to safety standards (see page 22). Some, however, do comply or can be amended to do so. This one did meet the standards, though we still replaced the hardware (metal springs and side pieces) to ensure safety.

After the most important items were in place, there was money left over to add a few other pieces: a side table, an inexpensive rag rug, and, for a bit of Old World elegance, a needlepoint footstool. Old needlepoint samplers can often be purchased at flea markets for $15 to $30, then made into footstools, framed, or made into pillows for a few dollars more.

Even though the couple had been told that their baby was a girl, they know that gender mistakes are sometimes made when an ultrasound is the source of the information. So as not to take any chances, they chose a gender-neutral color scheme based on cream with green accents. After the baby arrives, there'll be plenty of time to add some feminine or boyish flourishes.

opposite: Lack of closet space made this armoire a must. Look for one with adjustable shelves that you can change to suit the room's changing needs. Operating on the notion that babies like to look at other babies, we hung a series of baby photos over the crib. If you don't have pictures of yourself as an infant, look for vintage photos at flea markets and have them artfully framed. above: Old wire baskets provide a convenient place to stash toys and other extras. right: A side table was placed next to the rocker to make it easy for a nursing mom to have everything she needs at her fingertips. The window was hung with two types of curtains: a filmy set to let light filter in and ones made of thicker fabric that will darken the room.

dressing up an old dresser

Dressers are first and foremost functional. They need to hold plenty, be sturdy, and operate properly: There's nothing worse than having to struggle with a rickety drawer, particularly if you're a six-year-old or are holding a squirming infant. But dressers are often also a visual focal point in a bedroom, so you want to choose one that, if it doesn't start out beautiful, can at least be made to look attractive.

Hand-me-down and flea-market dressers have their pros and cons. On the plus side, older pieces often have carvings and interesting details that their newer counterparts lack. Because they're generally made of solid wood, they're also more substantial than more contemporary dressers, many of which are made out of particle board and veneer.

On the down side, the drawers in older pieces can be warped and difficult to slide in and out. Sometimes, too, old dressers have a lot of dye in the wood, which bleeds through when you try to repaint them. Still, most of these problems can be overcome.

Redoing a dresser is fairly simple. Here is the play by play:

1. Repair any drawer problems. If a drawer sticks, first try the simplest solution: Remove it from the dresser and wax the runner by rubbing it with a candle or bar of soap. If it still sticks, try sanding the areas that look uneven. Sometimes you'll find that the runners are damaged; if so you may need to remove them with a saw and replace them with new pieces of wood (bring in the old runners and have new ones cut for you at a home center or lumber yard).

2. Prepare for paint. Remove the hardware. If the dresser is peeling or flaking, you will need to strip it of its original paint. This is not a very pleasant process since it requires using a solvent. However, there are solvents on the market now that are less toxic than their predecessors, which could only be used with gloves and a mask. Ask at your local hardware store for the safest stripper available, but take precautions no matter how benign it appears. Never strip furniture when you're pregnant. Make sure you do it in an open, well-ventilated place.

3. Smooth the finish. If the piece you're redoing is in very bad shape, sanding may be all it requires to prepare it for painting. If the dresser has a glossy finish, you'll need to sand it down to create a surface for primer and paint to stick to. Start with a rough paper, then progress to a finer grade. Vacuum, then wipe with a cloth to remove all dust.

4. If you like, add architectural details. Glue on molding to give the piece an antique look.

5. Prime and paint. Apply a coat of primer to the dresser. If the original finish bleeds through, you'll need

to add another coat or two. Once the primer dries, go ahead and paint, using an oil-based paint (the piece will be easier to clean if you use oil versus water-based paint). Apply at least two coats, more if the color isn't true.

6. Replace or clean the hardware. If you'd like to change the hardware, now's the time. If you're keeping it, sand off the old paint and repaint it with paint made specifically for metal, or use an antiquing solution. (For more on hardware, see page 103).

7. Line the drawers. Use contact paper or old wallpaper to line the drawers before you fill the dresser.

from baby to **big boy**

When the time comes to put away the crib, parents can't help but feel a certain wistful twinge. But if the emotional part of transitioning a nursery into a toddler's room is hard, the actual work involved shouldn't be. A few small adjustments should be all it takes.

My son Eli's room is rather small, which in some ways made "growing it up" all the easier. Because of space limitations, I had restricted the room's furnishings so there weren't many pieces for him to outgrow. It also helped that I chose furniture that I knew could easily be updated.

As Eli neared age three, the first thing to go was his crib. But instead of replacing it with a standard twin, I chose to go with a junior-size bed—an option you might consider if your toddler's room is tiny. Granted, this will require eventually passing it down to his sibling and getting a new bed when he's bigger (and in a bigger room), but it was a small sacrifice to make considering I didn't have to change much else in the room.

In fact, I only replaced one other big piece: the rocking chair, which was swapped for a child-size club chair with ottoman, upholstered

Family heirlooms have to start somewhere. I designed Eli's crib specially for him and plan to pass it on to him to use for his own children. My mother and I sewed the cathedral quilt bumpers during my pregnancy. A clothes stand tucked into the corner turns wasted space into a storage opportunity.

above: A simple pad turned this dresser/cabinet into a changing table. Since the room is small and storage space at a premium, I designed it to have both convenient shelves and drawers. below: With the changing pad off, there's now room for a display of toys and a memory box. I also replaced some items on his bookshelf to create a more grown-up display.

Squares of vintage fabric with a sports motif were made into a duvet for Eli's new "big boy" bed. The Humpty-Dumpty lamp was traded in for a standing lamp, and art was hung on the wall where the crib sides used to be.

partly in leather. Originally, the rocking chair provided a wonderful spot for me to sit while nursing or reading to Eli. But as he grew and started looking at books by himself, I thought he'd be better served by a little chair of his own.

Some of the changes you'll make as your child grows will probably have more to do with accessories than furnishings. All those silver and stuffed baby gifts can be put away and items that better reflect your child's developing interests can be put in their place. When we converted Eli's changing table into a dresser—by taking off the pad and switching the doodads on top—we also packed away the antique toy collection on the shelf above and replaced it with vintage trucks. Eli's favorite toys are trucks and, as it happens, I had been collecting antique ones for several years, just waiting for the right place to display them. Though he knows they are not for play, he enjoys looking at them.

During the room makeover, we also made some practical alterations. Certain accessories that work fine in a baby's room only spell trouble when your toddler becomes more physically accomplished— and intensely curious. When Eli started to pull the Humpty-Dumpty bedside lamp into his crib and play with it, we knew it had to go. Replacing it with a standing lamp made the room safer and provides the room with more light.

In the end, Eli the toddler's room doesn't look all that different from Eli the baby's room, which was just what I had in mind: Enough changes were made to meet his growing needs and interests, but the room is still a familiar comfort zone— for both of us.

left: Eli loves his new bed. opposite: This room couldn't accommodate a tall bookshelf, but a short, elongated one fits neatly under the windows and holds nearly as many books and toys. An aquarium was added to the mix after Eli's second birthday.

boy or girl? gender-neutral design

When I was pregnant, I decided not to find out the sex of our baby. You might presume that made it difficult to furnish what would ultimately be Eli's room. As it turned out, that wasn't the stumbling block. Although I had spent the previous eight years designing nurseries for clients and friends, when it came to designing one for my own son, I was slightly flummoxed! Believe it or not, I found it harder to make decisions regarding the colors, fabrics, and furniture for my own home than for others'.

Ultimately, I created a room that would work for either a boy or a girl. As it happened, when I was four and a half months pregnant, I stumbled on a wonderful rooster quilt and I used it as a jumping-off point. I picked up its eggnog yellow, dusty green, and rich burgundy hues in the walls, furniture, and accessories, adding a little blue to round out the palette. (I think blue always looks great in either a girl's or a boy's room.) There are plenty of colors, fabrics, and furniture styles that are gender neutral. If you're uncertain about the sex of your unborn child, start with those and, if you like, add girlish or boyish touches after the baby is born.

overleaf left: Eli and I spent hours in this rocking chair. I had come across the rooster quilt on the back before he was born and used it to establish the palette for the room. A lack of storage space in my own room led me to annex Eli's closet, but an armoire fitted with shelves and a hanging rod was sufficient for his small garments. overleaf right: The rocking chair has given way to a small club chair of Eli's own, and the table is now primed for Lego play. Armoire doors provide a handy place for a chalkboard, hung at toddler height.

3 problem solving

Every room has its pluses and minuses. Bad light, but a good floor plan. Lofty ceilings, but a cramped closet. Add to that the challenges posed by the unique individual occupying the room (an avid doll collector, say, or a passionate Lego builder) plus assorted design ideas (Country French, perhaps, or a nautical theme) and you have your work cut out for you.

Although each room in this book provides its own set of obstacles, in this chapter we tackle four in particular: the oversize room, the small room, the room with storage difficulties, and the room shared by siblings of disparate ages. Sometimes it seems easier to ignore a room's problems and just make do. But by using some design tricks and putting some organizational ideas to use, I believe you can solve just about any dilemma. Nothing is going to turn a dinky bedroom into a palace, but you can certainly expand its storage capabilities and give it an airier feel.

If you've just moved into a new house or are creating a room for an unborn child, it pays to take some time and really antici-pate what the room's difficulties may be before you begin to fur-nish it. Will it have enough light—or too much? Are there awkward nooks and crannies in the room that you might be able to put to use for storage? Considering the room's size, what should be the scale of the furniture you buy?

All the rooms in this chapter were imperfect in at least one significant way, but each also had a fairly easy solution. Eventu-ally, the flaws even came to seem almost endearing, a good part of the rooms' ultimate charm.

little girl, big room

Can there be such a thing as a room that's too big?

Most people—particularly those who've had to shoehorn their children into closet-size boudoirs—would say no, but I can say from experience that big rooms can pose some very challenging problems. Such was the case with Gracie's bedroom, home at first to an infant, and now the domain of a rambunctious three-year-old.

A bedroom with an attached playroom/sitting area, Gracie's room has the breezy yet cozy feel of a summer cottage. But, pre-makeover, its size threatened to swallow up its tiny tenant. It needed some touches that would keep it light and airy (since the room stretches across the house, it receives natural light all day long) while making it warm and inviting, too. Several strategies helped accomplish that mission, but it all began with the wallpaper.

Gracie's mother, Kathy, had seen the fanciful topiary wallpaper and picket-fence border years earlier, and had vowed to buy it if she ever had another child. As it turned out, it was the perfect choice: The wallpaper's white background keeps the room bright, while its playful pattern visually "shrinks" the expansive space. Next came the painted plaid floor, which provided an easy way to break up a yawning breadth of hardwood and add whimsy to the room. All it took was a few good coats of paint. A pretty hooked rug breaks up the space even more and, though it adds another pattern to the mix, the room is big enough to handle it.

It would have been a mistake, however, to think that because the room is big, it could handle a ton of furniture. While it's human nature to want to fill

opposite: **Opting for a clover-shaped ottoman over a more traditional table gave this room a shot of humor and helped make it a comfy spot where the whole family likes to hang out and read or watch a movie. A TV and video collection are hidden in the armoire.** above: **Gracie's mother made this ribbon board to display family photos. The table beneath it was found in an antique shop—it was repainted and distressed to give it the patina of age.**

With a striking wicker bed as its focal point, Gracie's room needed little more in the way of extravagant details. A simple stuffed chair slip-covered against spills, a painted wooden blanket rack, a hamper, and shelves round out the rest of the furnishings. The bed, initially used by a nanny, has been in the room since day one.

up all the space we're allotted, I encourage clients to resist stuffing an oversize room with furniture. Here, the focus instead was on selecting a few fine pieces and placing them wisely.

In the sleeping area, for instance, the furnishings were kept relatively minimal. The big exception: a grand, curvaceous wicker bed that would overwhelm most kids' rooms, but is right at home in this space. In fact, its ample proportions help make the room seem snugger, as does the strategic decision to "float" the bed away from the wall. Positioning it where it's backlit by the windows also accentuates the bed's uncommon beauty.

Some of the same tricks help make the play area and sitting room cozier. A floating seating arrangement—two stuffed chairs and an ottoman that doubles as a table and comfy seat for Gracie's guests—has made the room so welcoming that it's become a favorite gathering place for the whole family.

Much of this room's appeal comes from a palette of simple colors and a mix of complementary patterns. The room really only has three colors—pink, white, and green—and the fabrics are a good mix of fun and fancy. The French toile used throughout the room might seem awfully grown up for a little girl, but when mixed with florals, gingham, and animal motifs, it helps bring the whole room together. And there's little in this room that Gracie will outgrow; it's likely to suit her well into her teenage years.

above: Shelves above a changing table provide a convenient place for accessories, distractions for the eye, and toys to calm a fretful baby. The changing table itself is really just a dresser with a padded top that can be removed when diapers are no longer needed.

how to make a big room more cozy

- A big room will swallow up small furnishings and details, so think big from floor to ceiling. In a large room, even moldings and baseboards can be oversize.

- Long walls can provide space for several pieces of furniture, but resist the urge to clutter them up. Instead, choose a few distinctive, multipurpose pieces. For instance, instead of putting a desk, bookshelf, and dresser on one wall, choose a large cabinet or shelving unit with drawers that provides all three built into one.

- Create a room within a room by making a separate play or seating area. Use rugs or even floor paint to help define its boundaries.

- Downsize a room with boldly printed wallpaper or by painting the ceiling a few shades darker than the walls.

- Use throw rugs or painted motifs to break up a broad expanse of floor.

- Try floating furniture; when everything is pushed against the walls, it can leave a great, gaping "hole" in the center of the room.

opposite, top: In a toddler's room, shelves that hold fragile collectibles like these glass figurines and fruit should be placed up high, well out of reach. A rack with oversize pegs—perfect for an oversize room—is a great way station for clothes when you don't have time to put everything in its right place.
left: Recessed built-in shelves are ideal next to a cozy window seat.

shipshape

Most kids these days have a lot of stuff, but some kids are natural-born collectors. Often, they'll latch onto one thing. In the case of Jeremy, age eleven, that thing is Lego. Jeremy has been amassing Lego sets since he was tiny and he is a fabulous builder who creates interesting structures both large and small. All that Lego, though, can strain a room's storage capacity, especially when that room doesn't have much storage space to begin with.

It's hard to complain about a bedroom set in a crow's nest overlooking the Pacific Ocean—especially one that has five windows affording a spectacular view and rounded walls that make it feel like it's on a ship. Still, the surplus of

opposite: Still ape for this stuffed monkey, Jeremy sleeps with it every night. above: Yo ho ho: Pillows with nautical motifs make the bed work as a sofa.

windows and curve of the room leave little space for large shelving and cabinet units, let alone clothes dressers. And because of the room's rounded shape, the closet is awkwardly configured.

The first thing I suggested Jeremy's mother, Paula, do was bring in a specialist to turn the closet into a workable storage space. While you might be loath to spend the money on a closet professional, it's really worth the expense. Having a closet that is well ordered helps kids take better care of their clothes and will give you peace of mind every time you open the door.

Making Jeremy's closet workable freed up an armoire that had previously been used to house his clothes. To make the piece Lego-friendly, we put dividers in the drawers, which keep the Lego bricks separate from his other toys and games. Lego pieces were also organized in baskets of varying sizes so that they could be stacked one on top of the other. We also had Jeremy's Lego in mind when we nestled a few low shelving units and a small cabinet beneath the windows: They provide a spot for him to show off his constructions (and, not incidentally, keep them off the floor).

Once the storage problems were solved, we could turn our attention to the fun part: taking advantage of the room's remarkable location. Taking a cue from the ocean below, a mural of a pirate ship was painted above a sleigh bed (with a trundle for friends), selected for its boatlike feel. The maritime theme was then extended to the pillows on the bed and on the desk chair.

We first decorated this room for Jeremy when he was seven, and his mother reports that he still loves it. He can frequently be found tucked away in his nautical nest doing homework, painting (another passion), and, of course, crafting those inventive Lego creations.

opposite: Jeremy's portrait of painter Claude Monet overlooks his Lego sculptures. top: Kids usually have to break down their creations since there's no place to put them. This room was designed with extra display space to give Jeremy the option of saving some of his constructions. above: Antique decoy fish rest on a window ledge.

top: A bedside table holds before-sleep reading and Jeremy's collection of soccer, baseball, and martial arts trophies. above: A mix of receptacles on Jeremy's desk keeps his pens and pencils handy. left: Dividers were built into the drawers of an armoire so that Lego pieces could live comfortably with other toys. opposite: When his desk gets overwhelmed with stuff, Jeremy (with pal Libby at his side) often pulls out the built-in "breadboard" on the side and turns his chair to work. Old and new: A toy schooner rests atop the computer.

good things
(in small packages)

There's something cozy about a tiny warren, especially when it's filled with little-girl stuff. Of course, when a small room is filled to the brim with little-girl stuff, it's not cozy, it's chaotic. Small rooms may have their charms, but it's essential to plan them wisely and to build in ample storage.

This was particularly true for Lizzy's room, as this five-year-old is an avid collector of dinosaurs. This is a girl who knows her Pachycephalosaurus from her Eoraptors. Fortunately, we found the perfect place to display the bulk of her collection, along with many of her books and toys. Despite its small size, Lizzy's room had two side-by-side closets on one wall—more, really, than was needed to accommodate her wardrobe. To make better use of the space, one of the closet doors was removed and the recess was fitted with shelves. Now, what would have been stored out of sight is out in the open, adding color and life to the room—without taking up an inch of extra floor space the way a free-standing bookshelf would.

Another way to save floor space in a small bedroom is to place all of the furniture flush against its perimeter. In this room, tucking the chair into the corner and pushing Lizzy's bed against the wall left a nice open rectangle of floor

opposite: After Lizzy's mother fell in love with a child-size club chair upholstered with a mix of new and vintage fabrics, we used it to set the tone for the rest of the room, using what was left of the bark cloth to trim the bedding and window treatments. above: Shelves, placed where a closet once stood, make way for Lizzy's dinosaur collection. You can add whimsy to shelves by gluing on "dingle balls," as was done here, or other types of decorative edging, such as rickrack or strands of beads.

1 Hide storage containers under the bed. Even if they'll be hidden behind a dust ruffle, choose attractive baskets and crates so you don't have to look at plastic boxes when they get pulled out onto the floor.

2 Opt for an armoire. If you lack closet space (or have no closet at all), an armoire is a lifesaver. Buy one that offers both double hanging space and drawers with an adjustable shelf option for later use.

3 Place the bed against the wall. Beds that extend into the room take up precious floor space that is better used for play. Situate the bed flush against the wall, then dress it up with pillows so that during the day it also functions as a sofa and provides a comfortable place for parents and child to sit and have some quality quiet time.

4 Use mirrors. Mirrors make a space look bigger, but instead of mirroring closets or hanging big full-length mirrors, create a group of several etched antique mirrors (see page 105). A less expensive alternative: Buy old frames at a flea market for as little as five dollars, paint them, then have them fitted with mirrors.

5 Go easy on patterns and colors. While you can still mix fabrics and colors in a small room, the calmer you can keep the design—by going, say, for a monotone look—the bigger the space will seem.

6 Keep window treatments simple. Big billowy curtains intrude into a room, taking up precious space. Go for Roman shades or blinds in neutral colors, using valances for accents if you like.

7 Make a place for everything. Little rooms tend to get overwhelmed with toys quickly, so good storage options are a must. While it may seem that one toy box may work better in a small space, the reality is that kids can never find what they're looking for in a big box and end up dumping out everything onto the floor. Have boxes or baskets for each type of toy and line them up against the wall or slide them into a bookshelf.

space where she can play. Allowing some pieces to do double duty—the dresser also functions as a bedside table—helped save space as well.

While small rooms benefit greatly from space-expanding strategies, it helps, too, if you pay attention to the details that give the impression of more space. For instance, to add a bit of girlishness to the room—but without adding frilly curtains, which would have made the room claustrophobic—I suggested simple shades set off by swags of fabric at the window tops. The valences, made from pink-striped ticking and punctuated by barkcloth bows, are a pretty addition but don't intrude into the room. Painting most of the furniture in light tones also helped give the room an airier feel. Although darker colors make nice accents for dinky spaces—here, lush green—used liberally, they can make the rooms seem even smaller.

Even when you employ a number of space-saving strategies and visual tricks to open up a small room, you'll still have to contend with the inevitable problem of where to store all of a child's playthings. The first place you'll probably look to is under the bed. We did that here, but rather than just stash a bunch of toys behind a dust ruffle, we placed everything in crates so it's easier for Lizzy to find what she's looking for. More crates and baskets, placed in corners and against the wall, help keep the space clutter-free. Sure, Lizzy's room isn't Brontosaurus-size, but it's a room that the young dinosaur aficionada is glad to call her own.

top: **To beautify standard-issue cloth-lined baskets, we painted them pastel colors. The wedge-shaped book rack, a thrift-shop find that was probably originally used to hold plates, fits snugly into the corner, saving space.** above: **Hat stands too beautiful to cover up with hats.**

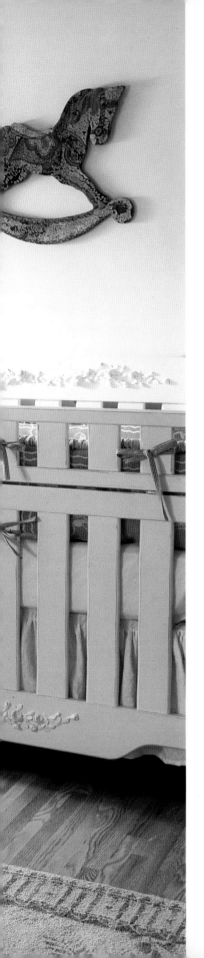

share and share alike

Shared bedrooms make for fond memories.
Many adults look back affectionately on the nights they lay in the dark talking to their siblings when they should have been fast asleep, the pillow fights, the parallel jumping on beds, the hours spent sprawled out on the floor listening to music. Not that relations are always so cordial when children share a room; there inevitably are fights over whose space is whose and the way that sharing makes a child's things—the things she considers hers and hers alone—so much more accessible to her sibling. Yet, for the most part, sharing a room is a wonderful experience for kids—and that's especially true when the room is designed with an eye to keeping things fair and square.

That objective can prove particularly tricky when the siblings are fairly far apart in age. In this room—a room that had belonged solely to five-year-old Siena for most of her life, but would now be home to her sister, ten-month-old Kayla, as well—the challenge was to create a space amenable to both a kindergartner and an infant. Siena didn't mind having her sister join her; in fact, she'd been asking for months when the baby was going to sleep in her bedroom. Nonetheless, it was important that the room still feel like her own special hideaway even though it would now be shared.

Any time you make over a child's room, whether it be to accommodate a sibling or just to give it a different look, letting the child have some input in the design can ease the transition. Here, Siena contributed to the fabric choices and weighed in on the room's colors. Like a lot of five-year-old girls, she had a strong preference for pink.

The small table in the center of the room can be easily moved to the side when the girls want space for floor play. Kayla's crib was chosen for its beauty and practicality—since it turns into a day bed, she'll be able to use it for years.

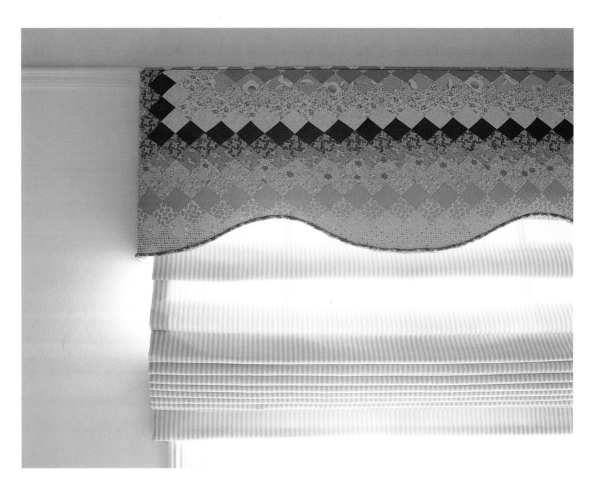

Previously, Siena's room had been put together piecemeal, using some furnishings that the family already owned and others purchased as needed. But Kayla's arrival seemed like the perfect time to give the room a more cohesive look and to bring in furnishings that would accommodate both girls.

Central to the room now are two yellow bookshelves—one for each girl—separated by a combined dresser and changing table to clearly mark the divide. To oblige Siena's penchant for pink and give her a piece in the room that's exclusively hers, we also brought in a desk with scalloped edging where she will eventually sit to do her homework. Right now she frequently spends time coloring and cutting up construction paper at the table-and-chair set, another recent addition that will, in time, become Kayla's domain.

One of the few "before" items that remains is Siena's iron daybed, a romantic piece that meshes well with the new furnishings. We did, however, add an array of pillows and change the bedding from a simple floral comforter to a patchwork duvet. The duvet cover is a unique design that recycles squares of chenille, vintage tablecloths, and other fabric remnants, some sewn into dress

opposite: A vintage quilt, too damaged to use on a bed, was turned into window valances and paired with Roman shades made from ticking. above: The great divide: Siena's shelving unit, on the left, holds books and playthings, while Kayla's, on the right, provides storage for blankets and stuffed toys. The changing pad is covered in soft chenille. right: Before Kayla moved in, the room was solely Siena's domain—with occasional visits from the family dog.

appliqués. In fact, many of the fabrics in this room are recycled. The valances, setting off Roman shades in pink ticking, are made from quilts that were too damaged to use as bedding. Likewise, the trunks I had made to provide additional individual storage for each girl are upholstered in more cut-up quilt and the remnants of an old chenille bedspread.

While some of the pieces in this room are identical —the two bookshelves, the upholstered trunks—not all of Siena's and Kayla's belongings match.

That's partly due to the gap in their ages, but it's also a design decision that can work even in a room for kids that are closer in years. In fact, furnishing a room with pieces that are complementary but not identical—beds made of the same wood with differently shaped headboards or dressers that match in color but not in height, for instance—can help each child feel that she has her own unique space.

In Siena and Kayla's room, once a retreat for one, now a haven for two, each girl has a lot to call her own. And that can only enhance the good times they'll have together.

top: Damask bumpers and a quilt create a cozy warren for the baby. left: Doors with little gingham curtains were added to the bottom of the shelving units to keep some toys out of sight. opposite: Wrap a corkboard in fabric and it loses that institutional schoolroom look.

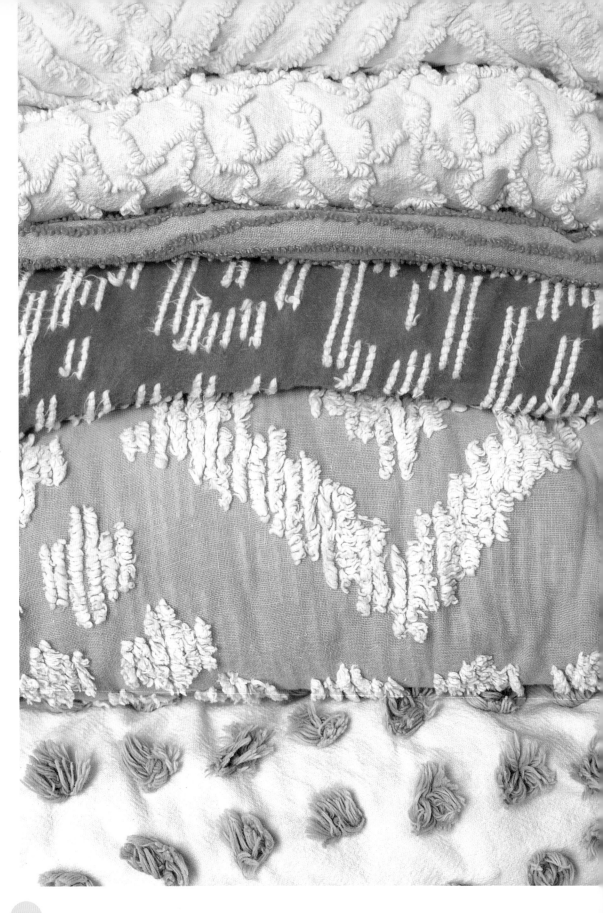

chenille chic

If chenille seems like the ideal fabric for a child's room, it may be because the person who invented the popular form of it was very nearly a child herself. Legend has it that Catherine Evans Whitener of Dalton, Georgia, was only a teenager when she created a tufting stitch that involved running stitches of yarn through fabric, then cutting it to make it fluff. In 1917, she and her brother founded a manufacturing company that later employed 10,000 hand tufters throughout the Depression. Chenille spreads became so popular in Georgia that merchants hung them on lines up and down a fifty-mile stretch between Dalton and Cartersville. The highway became known as "bedspread alley" and, because peacocks were the most prized motif, "peacock alley."

Chenille, of course, has other kid-friendly attributes besides its youthful creator. Tactile and squishy (chenille means caterpillar in French), the tufts of yarn invite kids to run their fingers through them. The best of the vintage chenille spreads feature bright colors with festive motifs: florals, cowboys, sailboats, animals, and geometric patterns to name a few. Subtler chenilles like white-on-white patterns or colored solids with wavy or crisscross designs appeal to a child's imagination, too—and can add a bit of playfulness to an otherwise subdued room.

From a parent's point of view, chenille is ideal because it's easy to care for: The spreads are colorfast and can just be thrown in the wash. When you shop for chenille, look for all-cotton spreads with lofty tufts and a strong background fabric. If you come across remnants of a chenille spread or one that's been damaged, snap it up. You can use it for pillows, upholstery, bibs, teething balls, window treatments . . . the possibilities are endless.

opposite: Chenille comes in almost every color and in a variety of patterns. These stacks from our factory are remnants waiting to be turned into pillows and upholstery. left: Vintage chenille turns an otherwise ordinary trunk into a beautiful box fit for storing dress-up clothes and soft enough to provide extra seating.

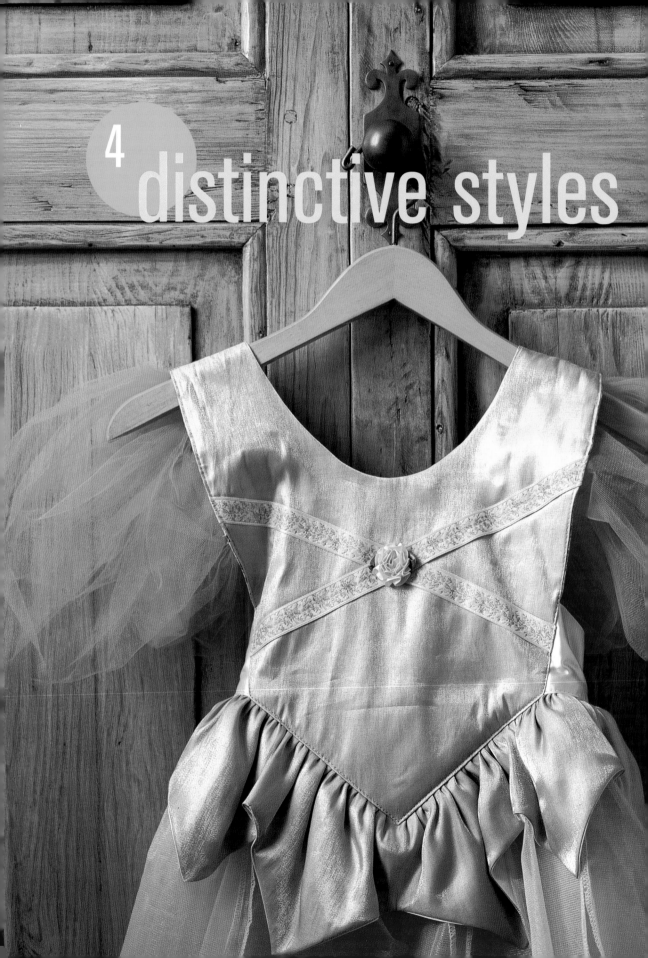

4
distinctive styles

Children develop their own sense of style early on. Why will one preschooler wear the same striped leggings day after day while her contemporary prefers a little velvet number? Why does one child want a picture of a white bunny on the wall while another wants a jungle scene? They make the choices for the same reasons that some adults like mid-century modern while others prefer farmhouse antiques: It's all a matter of taste.

Contrary to the old cliché, I do believe that there is some accounting for taste. In many cases, the style of home you grew up in will give you an appreciation for certain types of furnishings and accessories. Of course, some adults rebel completely against the style they grew up with. Bad taste has given birth to more than one interior designer running away from childhood memories. But if you take the time to incorporate your child's sense of style into the home, even if it's still in the developing stage, he will come to love his surroundings and take some sense of it with him into adulthood.

When the look you want to create is based on a particular style or theme, you're in for some fun. Hunting for just the right furnishings and gathering collections can be a real joy. One caveat: It's easy to go overboard with one style or theme. To prevent overkill, mix in a little of this and a little of that. A touch of eclecticism never hurt any environment and it's what makes your child's room different from anyone else's.

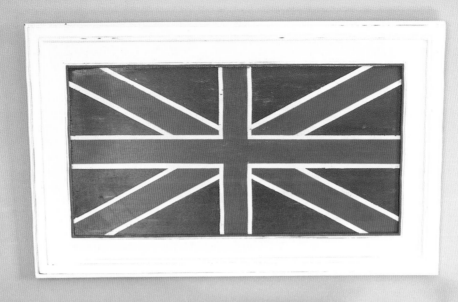

cross-cultural

You could choose among a hundred and one themes to infuse a child's room with personality, but perhaps none is as personal as a theme that reflects the family's heritage. Although the young denizen of this unabashedly boyish room lives in the United States, he has one parent who is British. My mission was to create a room that celebrated his cross-cultural lineage—and was warm and snug so he'd sleep tight at night.

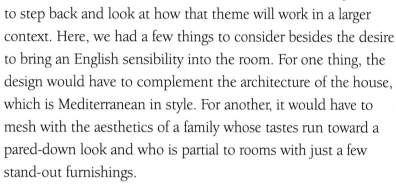

Any time you decide to design a child's room with a theme, it's important to step back and look at how that theme will work in a larger context. Here, we had a few things to consider besides the desire to bring an English sensibility into the room. For one thing, the design would have to complement the architecture of the house, which is Mediterranean in style. For another, it would have to mesh with the aesthetics of a family whose tastes run toward a pared-down look and who is partial to rooms with just a few stand-out furnishings.

With those factors in mind, we decided to keep the British touches few, but, as befitting a young boy, fun: a painting of a British flag above the bed, flag-stenciled storage boxes, and a clock and trunk adorned with more flags and guards from Buckingham Palace. To balance the other side of his heritage we also added a bit of Americana, including some vintage lunch boxes and a loveseat with an auto-racing motif in chenille.

Although this room is decorated simply, it hardly feels stark. Much of its warmth is owing to its periwinkle walls. White walls can be beautiful, especially when you want them to serve as a backdrop for various pieces of art. But colored walls add a certain warmth and life to a room that you don't get from white. In this room, in particular, the rich periwinkle gives the space a distinc-

opposite: In keeping with the sleek aesthetic of this room, we chose bedding that was as graphic as the flag hanging above it and kept the palette primarily to red, white, and blue.
above: Presently home to a big stuffed bear, this chicken-wire toy box has wheels and a pull so that a child (and his parents) can easily transport playthings from room to room.

tive look that makes it unnecessary to dress it with lots of extras—or ones that scream out for attention. The windows, for instance, are unobtrusively framed with graphic navy curtains punctuated with embroidered yellow stars. Likewise, the sconces are outfitted with shades that are restrained in design—though they still manage to inject a few lively shots of red into the room.

Each room in a house serves a different function above and beyond the obvious practical ones. With its soothing tones and comforting themes, this room isn't just a place for a little boy to sleep; it's a calming retreat where he'll most surely have sweet dreams.

opposite: A loveseat provides seating for more than one child—perfect for a little boy with a big sister who might want to share a book or two. The seat and back cushions are upholstered in remnants of a vintage chenille bedspread.

right: Time will tell: All the theme motifs in this room were confined to accessories like this clock, making it easy to switch styles as the child grows. A New York Yankees cap hung under the British flag is a reminder of this boy's dual ancestry.

below: Who ever thought those clunky lunch boxes we carried to school would become collector's items? Here, a few oldies but goodies decorate the dresser and cabinet above.

french twist

The beauty of doing a room in a particular style, whether it be Western-influenced or boldly modern or, like here, Country French, is that it helps you narrow down your choices, making decisions easier. The danger of doing a room in a particular style is that the room can ultimately look overdone. My philosophy for avoiding the latter is to adhere loosely to the chosen style and insert elements that "go" but, more important, express the personality of the family who'll be occupying the rooms.

This room, which now belongs to three-year-old Hayley, was originally going to be a guest room, designed to evoke the feeling of a French country inn. But no sooner had an antique iron bed and some vintage fabrics I'd found at a flea market been purchased for the room than it was discovered that Hayley was on the way. That meant that some of the plans for the space had to be changed, but not the Country French style at its heart. With its hallmarks of curvy furniture and mellow floral fabrics, Country French has a feminine look that is well suited to a little girl's room.

For the first couple of years, the double bed, initially used by a baby nurse, shared space with a crib. Since Hayley's boudoir is not particularly big, that left room only for a bedside table, which we painted in an antique French style; a slipcovered rocking chair; and an armoire for storage. (A changing table was placed in the bathroom across the hall.)

While most of the furniture in the room was newly bought, the armoire was

left: **Close inspection reveals some surprises in this Country French room: an iron bed with castings painted deep blue, a departure from the more expected all-white style; a cushy upholstered chair that looks staid but is actually a rocking chair; and animal-patterned lace curtains that are far from traditional.** above: **An armoire already in the family was revamped with shelves to provide storage space. The wire baskets, bought for pennies, were painted pink.**

a hand-me-down from Hayley's father—and a perfect example of how to rethink and recycle a piece. Originally, it seemed impractical for the room, since Hayley already had a substantial closet with a dresser built inside. But she did need space for her dolls, books, and toys, so we freshened up the armoire with a new coat of paint and built shelves inside. That eliminated the need to hunt down a new piece of furniture—and provided a way to install something with sentimental value in the room.

Key to this room's provincial style are the walls. What looks like a striped and floral wallpaper is actually a painted pattern, a subtle but stunning trompe l'oeil effect achieved by my friend Germaine Burke, whose forte is specialized interior painting. Since the room's ceilings are so high, we also installed molding to "frame" the walls and make the room cozier, and we had Germaine paint it to match the other details in the room.

As Hayley has grown, her room has evolved. On her first birthday, Hayley's parents gave her a tiny table and chairs, similar to a set I'd designed for the movie *Father of the Bride II*. When the crib came out of the room, the table and chairs were moved into its place, along with a small rocking chair. Neither addition is typical of the Country French look, but because they have a quiet femininity and grace, they blend in well.

One of the lessons to be learned from this room is that sweet needn't be saccharine and that girlish doesn't have to be garish. Confining the colors mostly to muted yellows, pinks, and blues and juxtaposing busy florals with the calming influence of natural wood has kept the room from looking over-the-top French. Instead, it's a warm environment in which a young girl with a penchant for princess dresses and tea parties can happily pursue dress-up and play.

top: Little Miss Muffet: a tufted stepstool provides both a hoist up to the bed and a soft place to sit.
opposite: A pint-size table and chairs in Hayley's room provide a place for tea parties and coloring. Painted light, light pink, they demonstrate that a girl's favorite color doesn't have to be cloying.

rural chic

These days, most parents make a grand effort to immerse their children in books. But the parents of John, age three, and Matt, age two, took that idea one step farther. By deriving inspiration from *The Little Red Barn* for the design of their sons' bedroom, they *literally* immersed John and Matt in one of the family's favorite books.

As it happens, the boys' room actually was somewhat barnlike in appearance to begin with. A high, peaked ceiling and exposed beams give the space the same loft-like feel as a barn, and the floor-to-ceiling window is even shaped like a barn door. That set the stage; all we needed was to add a few elements that capture the playful spirit of the children's beloved book.

Our goal, though, was to keep things simple since, as the boys grow and their preferences change, farm animals might quickly become too babyish. So we stuck to accoutrements that can easily be traded out later on: pillows and quilts with sweet farm animal and barn appliqués, a farm menagerie lamp, several framed rural-scene prints, and a small rug with a barnyard scene. Taking care not to oversaturate the room with *Little Barn* paraphernalia, we balanced the theme items with patchwork-quilt pillows and a big braided rug—textiles that resonate with the same nostalgia, but didn't cause barnyard overkill.

left: All rooms, even big ones like this, can use a few space savers. Here, it's a big basket to hold the boys' shoes and a bench that, outfitted with bookends, does double duty as a shelf. A trundle under the bunk bed provides room for their sister, who likes to sleep in their room from time to time. Adorning the walls at the back of the room are a tennis racquet and a bat that belonged to John and Matt's father when he was a boy (the tennis racquet was used to win a city tournament). above: Attractive jars usually intended to store food or hardware keep tiny toys from getting lost.

Of no less importance in this room was creating a space that can be comfortably shared by two young boys. Since the room is fairly large, we were able to create individual corners for John and Matt so each of them can have his own special place to play. Using bunk beds also helped free up space for play and made room for a big Brio table. While bunk beds don't work in every room—if you have low ceilings, they can be very claustrophobic—this room's airiness made them perfectly suitable. Something else to keep in mind about bunk beds: Kids sometimes tire of them after a few years or they don't fit properly in a new house. We solved that potential problem by making the bunks detachable so the beds can also be used side by side.

John and Matt still love *The Little Red Barn* and the bedroom it inspired. But, naturally, they have plenty of other special books in their future. The fun now is in finding which one will touch off the design for their room's next incarnation.

top: Fascinated by utility vehicles, three-year-old John is an ardent lover of trucks, tractors, and anything having to do with construction. A fleet awaits outside the boys' bedroom door. above: A small shelf and barnyard rug define Matt's play corner. Lack of storage space for clothes prompted the creation of this padded window seat with two deep drawers. opposite: A basket provides a low table for a lamp, and a stepstool offers John a place to sit in his special play corner.

something old, something new

I love things from past eras. Besides the fact that
some antique furnishings are simply exquisite, every worn spot and aged
imperfection gives me the sense that I'm preserving tradition. I can't help
but wonder who owned these things before and what went on in their lives.
Occasionally, though, those who, like me, love old things have to concede
that sometimes new *is* better, particularly in a child's room. However, what
often works best of all is a creative mix of the two.

In fifteen-year-old Erin's bedroom, antiques and modern takes
on antique looks live comfortably side by side. For instance, one
of the most dramatic pieces she has is a French-style vanity from
her great-grandmother's era. The piece, painted a soft green, was
actually a writing desk that Erin's mother, Stacey, found, fell in
love with, and had a mirror made to go with. Since the vanity
had no chair, Stacey decided to use an upholstered stool she
already owned. It doesn't match exactly—but many might say
that's exactly its charm.

Other areas in the room also juxtapose new and old. Erin's
desk is an antique upon which a modern computer is very much
at home. The lamp on her vanity is old; the shade is new. The
window seat and its striped and floral cushions are recent creations; the music stand placed next to them—Erin has been playing violin for
five years—is from bygone days. Even the polished floors, which are stained a
beautiful ebony shade, have a contemporary look that's been accented with
old-time hooked rugs.

At the tender age of fifteen, Erin has already developed her own sense of
style. She's a thoroughly modern teenager—one has only to look at her collection of CDs to see that—but she also has an abiding appreciation for elegant
objects from yesteryear.

opposite: **In several rooms through the house, artwork is propped rather than hung for an
unexpected effect. The antique music stand, a $100 find, is in harmony with the dark wood of the
floor.** above: **Multicolored stones, etched by Erin at camp, adorn a windowsill.**

right: Often old hardware doesn't function as well as new, but you can get the same look, as here, with reproductions. Hanging on the knob is the bag Erin carried during her bat mitzvah, too pretty to hide away in the closet. below: Two miniature forms, one an antique and one a newer découpaged take on the theme, do double duty as objets d'art and a place to hang jewelry. opposite: Besides teaming old and new, this room combines romantic elegance (floral fabrics and the vanity's swirls and curves) with elements that are a nod to Colonial style (matchstick blinds and dark wood floors). Still, despite the mix of styles, the room, with its pared-down palette of light green, white, and pink, has a beautiful simplicity.

Lily

5 personal expression

When I walk into a family's home, I can generally learn a lot about its personality just by looking at the surroundings. On occasion, I'll visit someone's home and find that it doesn't really reveal anything about the owners. Not what they like, not what they do in their spare time, not what they find beautiful. Although I'm certain they have other means of expression, I always long to "read" their rooms.

Most kids' rooms, at least when the child is very young, say more about the parents than the kids. But that's to be expected. Not only do we design our children's rooms according to our own sense of style, but most of us also add in a drop of nostalgia and a good dollop of wishful thinking, in hopes that our children will like the same things we do.

That isn't to say that even the room of a young child can't offer some clues to his personality. It may be as simple as adorning your child's bedroom with the toys that he likes. Or going a step farther and picking out quiet—or more raucous—colors to match your child's temperament. If a young girl is very feminine, that's easily reflected with a girlish décor. Likewise, the room of a real boy's boy can be festooned simply with lots of familiar boyish trappings.

Naturally, as a child gets older he will develop his own ideas about his room. But that, I think, is when it gets fun. Let your child be your partner in design and together you can create a room that's both practical and personal—and, not incidentally, have a good time doing it.

planes, trains, and automobiles

One of the most rewarding aspects of parenting is watching your child's interests develop. There's no telling what young boys and girls will grow to like or whether they will become engrossed with how the real world works or more enthralled with fantasy. In either case, it's great fun to nurture their curiosity, and one of the best ways to do that is to create a room that features their individual interests prominently.

Hunter, the six-year-old occupant of this room, is a vehicles guy; he loves anything with an engine. With that in mind, his parents, who collect vintage advertising posters, bought a lighthearted old French automobile ad and let it set the tone for the rest of the room's design. For instance, they chose a bed that picks up the red in the poster (the picket-fence style was Hunter's call) and an upholstered chair that matches the poster's blue. In keeping with the vehicular theme, they hung painted metal airplane plaques on the wall and lined display shelves with antique toy trucks. A brilliant finishing touch: The drawer pulls on Hunter's dresser are made from trains bought at a toy store and then made into custom knobs at a hardware store.

Theme rooms can be wonderful—and they can be horribly over the top. What makes the difference here is restraint. There are plenty of trains, planes, and automobiles for Hunter to enjoy, but not so many that it looks like an amusement park. Opting for race-car pillows rather than, say, a race-car bed, or a flannel blanket with a train motif rather than a train mural, also will make it easy to "grow up" the room as Hunter's

Pillows, a bedroom staple, help give this room its boyish charm. The race car shams were made from vintage curtain panels; the pillows on the window seat boast a mix of sporty new and old fabrics. Storage space being at a premium here, cabinets were incorporated into the window seat and shelves were built into a decorative niche in the wall that would otherwise have been wasted space.

tastes change. In fact, they already have. As his enchantment with sports has grown, pillows printed with football players and a trunk embellished with a baseball diamond have been added. Eventually, his mother, Mary, also plans to replace the train pulls on his dresser with Matchbox cars, a nod to his increasing fascination with auto racing.

Finding clever ways to incorporate Hunter's interests into the room wasn't the only challenge here. Although it's an ample size, the room has little wall space owing to a surfeit of windows—a boon in terms of light, but bad in terms of storage. To circumvent the problem, a dresser was built into the closet and an armoire was customized to provide both a desk and storage space. This proved pivotal since Hunter, Mary reports, spends most of his free time on the computer. That is, when he's not jumping on the bed he picked out.

left: The doors in this armoire pocket in so that Hunter wouldn't bump into them when he was in the toddler stage. On top—an oft-forgotten storage spot—a collection of teddy bears sleeps peacefully. opposite: This bedside lamp, made from a fishing rod, was a $10 flea-market find.

easy hardware ideas

Pulls, knobs, and handles can make or break the look of a piece of furniture. As a long-time collector of old hardware, I love the glint of a crystal pull, the patina of an antique latch, and the worn look of a pull that has been painted over several times. It's the little details like these that make a dresser or armoire special and unique. Using beautiful old hardware is also a great way to add character to the simple pieces of unfinished furniture, popular because they're widely available at reasonable prices.

Some stores specialize in antique hardware and a variety of knobs and pulls can often be found at flea markets. Another option is to purchase reproductions, which can be equally beautiful and oftentimes more reliable than their secondhand inspirations. You can also buy new hardware and antique it yourself. Most paint stores carry antiqueing solutions, and the process is simple. Wearing gloves, soak the hardware in the solution according to instructions. Remove from the solution and allow to dry on a clean, paper-lined surface, then spray the hardware with a clear finish. This last step is essential, as it will keep the toxic chemicals of the antiqueing solution from getting on your hands.

Another way to make special hardware for your child's room is to have tiny toys—anything from toy soldiers to miniature trains to Lilliputian-size dolls—made into pulls at your local hardware store. As your child gets older, you can change the pulls to suit her changing interests. It's an easy and inexpensive way to help the room grow up.

opposite: Having some open shelves in a closet makes it easier for kids to find what they're looking for—and less likely to throw things on the floor the way they might when rummaging through a drawer.

the young romantic

What makes a girl's room a girl's room? Pink is the easy answer, but not necessarily the correct one. In fact, pink could be entirely absent from a room and you'd still know that its occupant was a Katie or a Madeline. From my perspective, a girl's room is one that may indeed have feminine colors and other traditional feminine trappings such as florals and lace. But, more important, it's a room that's dreamy, imaginative, and set up for a

girl to do the things that girls like to do. And often (though, of course, not always) that is different from what boys like to do.

Sydney, the four-year-old who occupies this garret, is, as her mother, Debbie, puts it, "total girl." She loves to play with Barbies, is a connoisseur of ballerina dresses, and, yes, gravitates toward the color pink. But as much as Debbie wanted a room for Sydney that celebrates her girliness, she also wanted a design that would see her daughter through many years to come—and in that case a frilly bauble of a bedroom wouldn't do. We settled on a romantic look that wouldn't be too sugary for a twelve-year-old, but was sweet enough to appeal to a four-year-old with definite likes and dislikes.

While there are all kinds of elaborate furnishings you can use to create romance in a room, I prefer to keep the furniture modest and add a fanciful mix of fabrics instead. On Sydney's bed, for instance, we combined six different fabrics, unified by like colors and a balance of big and small patterns. We

left: When it comes to wicker, don't just think white. This antique vanity has a far more powerful presence painted cranberry to complement the fabrics in the room. above: We saw antique mirrors hung salon style over a bathtub and thought it would look great in a bedroom, too. After searching unsuccessfully for the right mirrors, I made new ones and had them etched and antiqued at a glass store. Beneath the mirrors: glass lamps with crystal drops and the surprise of mismatched shades.

left: The furnishings in Sydney's room were kept simple so as not to compete with the mix of romantic fabrics. Although there is carpet on the floor, throwing a rug with a graceful pattern on top brings in more color and pattern. above: Rather than use a traditional dust ruffle, which would hide the bed frame, we attached a toile bedskirt with Velcro.

also used, to striking effect, double-width stretches of toile around the windows. Pulled to the side, the curtains make charming frames for the paned glass; closed, they create a fantastic expanse of pattern and color.

Rather than saturate Sydney's room with pink, I centered the room around a deeper, richer color: cranberry, a hue that is close enough to pink to appeal to a little girl, but not so pink she'll tire of it as she grows. Likewise, Sydney's furniture is made to suit her in both the present and the future. The shelving unit, made in the classic-French bombé style, is now filled with a preschooler's treasures, but it will look equally appropriate adorned with a teenager's collections. The wicker vanity, a great antique-shop find we painted to match the room, is perfect now for coloring and kid-preferred pursuits (it's been a big hit with Sydney's friends who come over to play dress-up). Later on, she'll use it for homework and, one day, even as a place to do her hair and makeup.

For a final touch of romance, we added a chaise longue. If you have a room sizable enough to handle a chaise, it's a great alternative to a club chair. Sydney uses it not only as a spot for looking at books, but also as a place to cuddle up when she's sick or upset. (Her parents call it the "drama chair.")

To the uninitiated, this romantic haven might seem mature for a preschooler, but both Sydney and her friends find it inviting. And as lovely as it is, there's nothing the kids can't lie on or touch. One day a friend of Debbie's, upon seeing Sydney's room, remarked, "I know a twelve-year-old who'd love this." Debbie's response? "Good. I want Sydney to like it when she's twelve, too."

opposite: Barbies from Sydney's collection have a time-out. above: Fabrics from Sydney's bed lend themselves nicely to this corner of the room, too. The chaise was slipcovered for easy washing and so that, should Debbie choose to replace the bedding in later years, it can be easily changed as well.

teenage kitsch

Children grow up way too fast, at least in the minds of their parents. In their own minds, of course, they can't grow up fast enough—and they often want their rooms to reflect their increasing maturity. Yet, at the same time, even kids right on the cusp of teendom can be reluctant to part with some of the objects that sustained them through childhood. The resulting clash of desires can be a real mishmash, a room that's neither here nor there. Fortunately, with a little finesse, it can be a lovely balance of contrasts.

Lily is a twelve-year-old who has a grown-up's taste for sophisticated furnishings and a young girl's penchant for funky collectibles and quirky souvenirs. Her room is a testament to both. With its subtly patterned wallpaper, sumptuous floral rug, hand-painted antique bed, and dainty slipper chair, the room is both refined and understated enough to complement (not compete with) the house's Tudor architecture. A pretty pink dresser—a flea-market find repainted and fitted with new hardware—floral sconces, and taffeta curtains add to the room's romantic feel.

The mix of disparate items in this room—antique bed, slipper chair, taffeta curtains juxtaposed with kitschy souvenirs of Hawaii and funky folk art—works well because everything is in proportion. The refined furnishings aren't so attention-getting that they drown out the more playful objects, and the witty accessories aren't so plentiful that they overwhelm the antiques.

But a closer look betrays Lily's playful side. A mirrored disco ball suspended from the ceiling lightens up the room's earnest elegance, and a collection of amusing souvenir plates from Hawaii hung on the wall reveals Lily's affinity for kitsch. For more punch, a wild leopard-print pillow is slipped onto a toile slipper chair and tongue-in-cheek folk-art paintings are hung above the dresser and propped on the desk.

Besides injecting Lily's personality into the room, these funky accessories keep it up to date without a major overhaul. The major elements of furniture, wallpaper, and curtains have been in the room since Lily was in kindergarten, and she's developed an appreciation for their beauty—even turning down a generous offer from her mother to redo the room in the modern style her friends prefer. But by continuing to amend the art and other incidentals, Lily can refresh the room regularly throughout the years to come. That way, it will always reflect a bit of both Lily the little girl and Lily the young sophisticate.

right: Where the wild things are: A leopard-print pillow gives this elegant toile-covered slipper chair youthful flair.
opposite: A personalized folk-art painting of Lily and her cat Toonces and a collection of Buddhas play off the weathered elegance of a painted flea-market dresser.

Lily,
Queen of
the House
and her cat
Joonces

opposite: Although its provenance is unknown, this vintage bed has the look of a nineteenth-century French piece. The jumble of florals here could easily have amounted to overkill, but since each design is subtle, they mix up just right. above: Since Lily's computer is in another room, her desk is given over to whimsical objects: a plain lamp made playful with the unexpected addition of a feather boa glued onto the lampshade edge; and folk art made with found objects—twigs, shells, and rocks—propped on the desk for close-up viewing.

6
playtime

Take a moment to wax nostalgic: Think back to the time when your home was not cluttered with art supplies, doll carriages, model dinosaurs, and puzzles. When you could walk through a room without picking your way through toy trucks and Playmobil castles, and sit on a sofa without feeling a few broken crayons. Now come back down to earth and face reality: You now have more stuff than ever to deal with.

Don't be discouraged. And don't give up on the idea that you can make a space that you share with your kids attractive and livable. As easy as it is just to give up and let your children's things dominate, I firmly believe it's possible to find a solution that makes both you and your kids happy. Ultimately, there can be room for everything and everyone.

In some cases this might mean equitably dividing the space. In other cases it might mean finding a way that your things and your children's things can live peacefully together while intermingled. In either case, adding elements to the room that make it easy to keep organized—and keep the peace—will help you tremendously.

If your child is fortunate, you may also have a room that you can dedicate solely (or at least halfway) to child's play—though what constitutes "play" is wide open. To one child it's doing puzzles and drawing, to another it's constructing buildings out of blocks. To still another it's dressing up dolls, and to her older sister it's stringing beads to make earrings and necklaces to sell.

The rooms on these pages are not your typical playrooms in that they aren't simply filled with toys. Some are rooms shared by both parents and children; some are rooms designed with a particular pastime in mind. Even if you're more interested in creating a traditional playroom for your child, you'll be able to borrow some ideas from these special rooms. The key is to find a happy medium between practical furnishings and those that also have a winning style.

the artists' atelier

Most kids spend hours and hours of their childhood creating art. And, whether a child is a budding Rembrandt or can barely draw a straight line, those works are usually masterpieces in her parents' eyes. But there's often a price to pay for such prolific creativity, whether it be spilled paint, crayon marks, or just the sheer clutter of art supplies. At the home of Shannon, age seven, and Rachel, age ten, the girls were always in the middle of one project or another on the kitchen table. When it came time for dinner, chaos would ensue as they scrambled to put away paintings-in-progress and other art paraphernalia. Their mother vowed that when they moved to a bigger house, she'd devote a room specifically to art.

The resulting art room is the girls' favorite place in the house and its practicality pleases their mother no end. We built a storage unit for the room that incorporates a sink for cleanup and a melamine counter that makes wiping up spills easy. (It also contains a keyboard drawer so that it can be converted into a computer desk at some point if the family desires.) The piece houses not only art supplies, but games and plenty of "junk"

With its sink, melamine counters, and Prego floors, the art room is designed for easy cleanup. Painted cherries on the storage unit give it a playful look and echo the fruit-motif fabrics on the window seat. The tufted ottoman in the foreground opens up for storage and a step stool helps the girls access up-high supplies.

right: Construction paper and other art supplies are stored in painted sap buckets. Paints are transferred to mason jars, which make colors easy to identify. The brush holder is made from chopsticks. below: In a small room, anything that can do double duty is a welcome addition. Here, the two ottomans make a fine resting place for Rachel's feet and a great place to store Shannon's collection of stuffed animals.

above, right: Oh, that the "junk" drawer pull were only tongue in cheek! In fact, just about every play-room needs a junk drawer. Here, it's labeled as such. opposite: The table can be pulled away to provide floor space for playing games. Under the window seat are shelves for books, puzzles, and games.

that is kept out of sight by cabinet doors. Some of the doors are actually window shutters bought at a home center and attached to the unit's upper shelves —a trick you can use on any shelving unit to create some enclosed space and break up uniformity.

The room also houses a large table that allows the young artists, who both attend art school, ample space for drawing, painting, and craft projects. Stools and a bench beneath the window provide comfortable seating for the girls and friends who come by to play and paint. The atelier, however, isn't just used for art. Rachel does her reading and homework in the room and a split closet door provides a place for Shannon to play store or create puppet shows. Occasionally, a set of parents can be found hanging out in the atelier, too. It's so comfortable that the whole family uses it as a place to relax.

room for imagination

When most of the balls and dolls
and trucks are gone, a playroom can be a sad
and empty reminder of the days when your children were still toddling about—and it seems like
just yesterday! Playrooms, like bedrooms, need
to change as kids and their interests change.
Sometimes they're best turned into study halls, a
place where kids can do homework undisturbed.
In this case, a playroom for two young girls, Erin
and Kyle, was reborn as a crafts room for two
young ladies, now fifteen and ten, respectively.

A second-story aerie, Erin and Kyle's crafts
room has windows spanning two walls, making
it feel like a tree house—a country tree house, if
you consider the furnishings. A large farm table
sits at the room's center, providing a place for
the girls to work. This type of table, especially
one with an unpainted top, is the perfect choice
for arts and crafts: Since it's already rough-hewn,
any stains or nicks it gets in the process of the
girls' work will add to, not spoil, its character.
For seating, I brought in painted stools, a better
option than chairs because of the table's height.

Erin, at work on one of her beaded handbags, turns out a
wealth of goods in the crafts room. Matchstick blinds keep the
aerie light but block the sun when necessary; stools in a mix of
shades make the seating area more interesting than monotone
ones would.

Perched under the room's longest set of windows is a storage piece that Erin and Kyle's mom picked up at an antiques store. It's the kind of find that's a revelation—fabulously practical, unique, and great-looking all at the same time. The piece was probably originally used to hold hardware in a factory or other type of industrial space. Now its drawers house the girls' supplies and its bins, some of their many books. The elongated top provides a place to show off a few of their creations.

Art is also exhibited on a double-wide corkboard with a frame that echoes the country feel of the room. Beneath the board, we placed a mantel that puts jars of beads and baubles within the girls' easy reach. Although it might seem odd to hang a mantel in the middle of the wall with no fireplace beneath, it works well here because it's not as deep as a shelf and seems like an extension of the corkboard.

Comfortable and well organized, the crafts room has lent itself not only to hours of fun, but to true industry. In the spirit of entrepreneurship, Erin, who makes whimsical handbags from cigar boxes, beads, and decals as well as skirts pieced together from vintage handkerchiefs, has already sold some of her wares to one of the toniest shops in town.

opposite: A combination chest and shelving unit covering one wall of the room provides storage space. The shelves were covered with old wallpaper I found in an antiques store during a trip to the Napa Valley.

above: Unearthed in an antiques store, this piece was originally used in a factory to hold tools and hardware. In a crafts room, it provides both expansive storage and a display area for the girls' handmade creations.

left: If you can't find an extra-wide corkboard or don't want to go to the expense of having one made, buy two wood-framed boards at a business supply store, paint the frames, and hang them side by side. below: Plain black-lidded jars as well as the kind of metal-topped vessels used in medical offices make excellent receptacles for beads and things. Painted-on labels won't fall off the way taped and glued-on ones often do.

fun for all ages

Although the difference between a boy who's twelve and a girl who's six is actually only six years, the age gap between a preteen and a first-grader can seem as wide as the Grand Canyon. Add in another boy and girl, ages eight and ten, respectively, and you have a group of children who are likely to have varying interests and needs. Is it possible for one playroom to suit them all?

In fact, in this basement playroom belonging to those four children, the offspring of Vicki and Jimmy Iovine, there's something for everyone. Part of that is owing to its size: there's enough space to accommodate the older son's drum set as well as dollhouses and superhero toys. And part of it is owing to the design of certain pieces of furniture. The shelf and cabinet unit, for instance, provides cubbyholes that can be individualized for each child's use. No less effective in making this room congenial is its gender-neutral design. Neither frilly nor overtly masculine, everything from the floor to the fabrics could work equally well in a boy's or a girl's room.

Another challenge facing us here was

A plain wooden table looks unremarkable until a peek underneath reveals legs made of unfinished logs. Lined with an art bulletin board, cartoon characters, and sports posters, the walls reflect the varied ages of this room's occupants.

that, since the family had only recently moved into the house, the playroom was to be furnished with lots of odds and ends from their previous home. Among those odds and ends were two large futons that we slipcovered and decked out with piles of pillows to create an ersatz sofa. Futons, as it happens, work well in playrooms since they're informal and nearly indestructible. (Futons are also a good alternative to a trundle bed: Store one under your child's bed, then slide it out for sleepovers.) We also slipcovered plastic chairs in plaid jewel-toned fabric to give them a more chic look.

While the slipcovering helped to give the room more style, the black-and-white check flooring also went a long way toward giving it some polish. The floor brightens the space, too, helping to obscure the fact that there are no windows in the room. It may be a basement, but the addition of color, graphic pattern, and warming fabrics ensures that it hardly feels like a dungeon. And while it can be a cacophony down there, with four children simultaneously drumming, watching videos, and taking part in games, having a suitable room to play in helps the Iovine family stay in harmony.

above: Kids' chairs often get scuffed, scratched, and dotted with paint and marker. Instead of buying new ones, consider having slipcovers made; they're washable and add polish to a room. opposite: Cubbyholes make it easy to designate space for each child, while cabinet doors allow some playthings to be stored out of sight.

the happy family room

The family room is the best of rooms—and the worst of rooms. On the one hand, it provides a place for parents and children to spend time playing together or even just going about their own business with the comfort of knowing the others are nearby. On the other hand, the family room is a place where "kid stuff" such as toys, art supplies, children's books, and videos poach from what adults would like to be their territory. Can this marriage of parents' and children's things be saved?

This cozy den is proof that it can. Originally, the room had a nice assemblage of plush upholstered furniture and a hardwood floor, but most of it lay buried beneath a jumble of playthings. It might seem odd, then, that we chose to add yet another piece to the room—in this case, a childrens' craft table. However, this additional element actually helped organize the room by providing the kids with a place to color and create. Now, when toys are left lying around, it's more often on the table and not underfoot as before.

The next step was to put the room's built-in cabinets to use. Instead of using a big box to store the kids' toys, we split them up into baskets and

Here, little things make a big difference. The children's art table has drawers for extra storage, and toys were put into baskets to keep open shelves neat. Since the space also functions as a guest room, the sofa, an unexpected combination of wood and soft pillows, has a foldout bed.

133

above: A picket fence provides a welcoming entrance to the family room and, when necessary, keeps the dog out.

opposite, top: Who needs fancy building materials? This elegant castle is made from a laundry detergent carton, Popsicle sticks, and construction paper. opposite: The kids' fire engines and trucks share space with their parents' sound system.

placed the baskets in the cabinets. That way, the toys aren't as likely to get shoved to the back where no one can find them or where they'll simply be forgotten. To keep the parents' gear separate from the children's, we assigned some shelves to the adults, others to the kids.

This family also benefited from the addition of a book rack. Aesthetically, book racks are a nice change from bookshelves, plus they make it easy for a young child to grab a book—and put it away. (Another family I know keeps their rack in the kitchen and stocked with reading material for both kids and parents.) In this case, the book rack does double duty, also hiding an unused fireplace.

As important as it is to find a place for everyone's stuff, a family room that makes everyone happy also needs to have a mood that's conducive to both relaxation (for the parents) and play (for the kids). Here we achieved that by using summery florals, pale yellows and greens to keep the room both bright and informal, and a needlepoint rug dark enough to hide dirt but not so dark that it dulls the room. As it should be, everyone in the household finds the family room inviting—even the dog and cat. Occasionally, the turtle, too.

family business

Home offices are often off-limits for children, but that doesn't necessarily keep them from wandering in and out or even plunking right down and making themselves at home. In our house, we solved the problem by turning our office into a shared space, with a desk for me and a play table for my son, Eli.

Although Eli sometimes uses the computer, I made a special effort to create his own special place in the room. That's given him a certain proprietary pride in his "office" and, thankfully, has helped lessen his interest in what's sitting on top of my desk.

The configuration of our office space made it possible to split it in half, with Eli's table on one wall and my desk on the other. If you have a room that doesn't divide as easily, you can get the same effect by carving out a corner for your child's table and playthings. But don't stop there. To set off Eli's space even more, I framed some of his paintings and hung them over his table. On a bulletin board placed just below the paintings, I tack up pictures that he likes as well as his own works in progress.

I also positioned two identical bookshelves in the office: one for Eli's art supplies and toys, and one to hold my personal and business items. Another bookshelf in the room is shared; since Eli can only reach the lower shelves, he gets three on the bottom for toys and books, while my belongings fill up the rest.

The divide between Eli's and my side of the office is filled with a hooked rug. The alternating log-cabin and floral pattern helps warm up the room and is busy enough to hide spills and stains—an inevitability when your officemate happens to be a three-year-old.

opposite: A collection of old child-size chairs makes what would have been dead space visually interesting, gives the room a more child-friendly feel, and provides seating for Eli's guests. above: My son and I share this double bookshelf: Eli gets the lower three shelves on the left, which keep his books and toys within his reach.

left: Storage space is maximized by placing a cubbyhole unit over the desk, a nice change of pace from regular shelving. Painted wire baskets and a ribbon board help keep things organized on and above the desk. above: Shelves are just one step toward getting organized. Using a variety of vessels to divide up odds and ends on top of shelves helps a room stay even neater. On Eli's side of the room I used galvanized metal bins painted soft colors, varying round and square wire baskets, and wooden crates.

the gorgeous garage

A gorgeous garage may seem like an oxymoron, and perhaps I do exaggerate a bit when I call this garage gorgeous. But too often we resign ourselves to the fact that garages are just a place to shove stuff, then pull down the door. It doesn't have to be a mess, though.

With four children in the family, the owners of this home found that the garage door was open as often as it was closed, making it difficult to overlook the clutter inside. First and foremost, the garage needed organization, but because it isn't used for cars—half of it is taken up by a room added on a few years back—we decided to make it a dual play and storage space.

Previously, the family's stuff had been haphazardly thrown into boxes, making it difficult for members to find what they were looking for. During the makeover, the boxes got the boot and we replaced them with inexpensive shelving units. Next we placed various containers on the shelves to help separate dolls from balls and other items. Large balls, bats, tennis racquets, hockey sticks, and other sports equipment were relegated to tall metal mesh barrels.

Since it's hard to make everything in a garage look neat, we hung a curtain to close off a section where bikes and other gear are stored. Nothing fancy—just a big piece of gingham slipped through shower-curtain rings, hung on a spring rod and accented with ribbon bows—the curtain nonetheless adds an unexpected decorative touch. Remember, there's no law that says a garage can't have visual appeal. Here, we added a drawing and tableau of old toys to dress up the space even further. Try rummaging through your own garage. Chances are you have several decorative items in boxes that can be used to create an attractive display.

With the previous jumble moved onto shelves, the garage now provided room for play, so we painted tic-tac-toe and hopscotch outlines on the floor. That brings the kids into the garage so often that the door almost never closes at all anymore. But since the space is neat and streamlined now, the family doesn't mind—and neither do the neighbors.

Wire baskets painted black keep art supplies, tools, and toys organized. A tableau of old toys beneath a drawing gives the garage some style.

left: Now that the garage is neat and clean, there's no need to keep the door closed. With family odds and ends relegated to shelves, there's room for tic-tac-toe and hopscotch on the floor. above: The simple curtain in the back hides tools, skis, bikes, and strollers not used on a daily basis. below: Balls and seashore collectibles peacefully coexist in separate wire baskets.

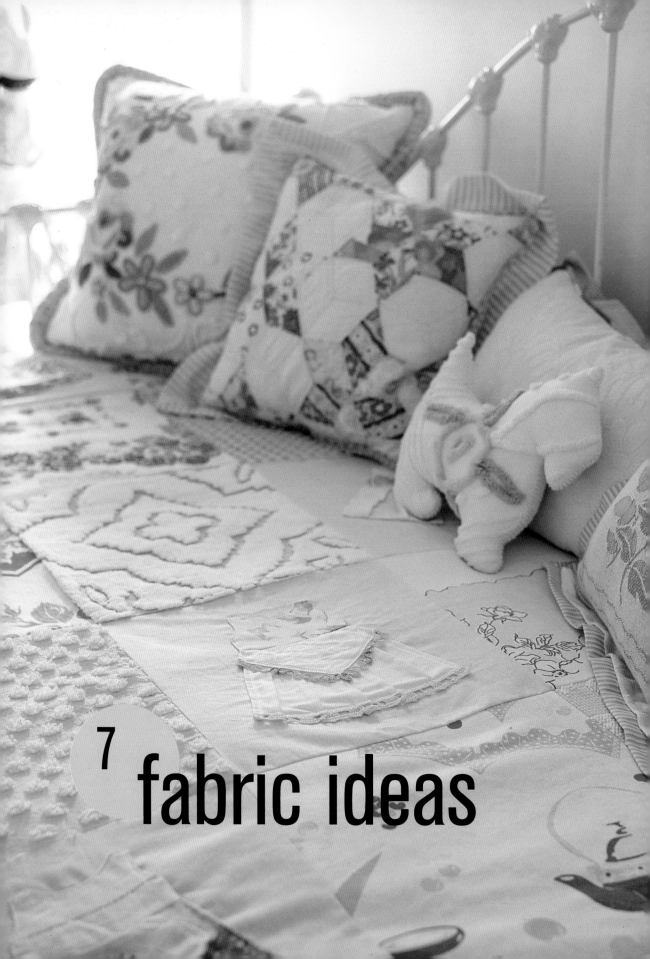

⁷ fabric ideas

As someone who designs furniture, I hate to admit that it's generally not the gentle curve of a chair back or the cleverly crafted legs of a table that draws our attention when we enter a room—it's the fabrics. The crazy mix of striped and plaid pillows piled high on a mattress; the cozy patchwork quilt thrown over the back of a sofa; layers of pink, cranberry, and cream floral linens tucked into a little girl's bed; unapologetically boyish curtains with a round-'em-up-cowboy theme framing the windows—they all catch our eyes long before we notice if the bed is made of iron or wood.

Textiles are the heart and soul of a room, and they touch children both literally and figuratively. A comforter should wrap your child with softness as it delights her with its beautiful pattern and colors. An upholstered chair should hold her in a warm embrace while at the same time perking up her room with color and texture. When well chosen, fabrics can be a treat to look at and touch.

What defines well chosen? There's no one type of fabric that is "right" for children's rooms. In fact, kids' rooms lend themselves to a wonderful mix of textiles, both vintage and new. I do, however, think that the fabrics that best accessorize any type of room are those made from natural fibers such as cotton, linen, and yes, even silk. These fabrics simply feel better against child-soft skin and, because they don't have a synthetic sheen, look better, too. I'm also partial to certain types of prints and patterns. I love the homespun look of tickings, the sturdy, stripey cotton used to cover mattresses. Another favorite is vintage bark cloth from the forties and fifties, a slightly puckered or nubby fabric that generally has a floral print, but is also found in abstract and cowboy motifs. The fabric's name stems from the fact that it once contained bark. Plaids, checks, ginghams, French-style toiles, denims, warm-hued solids, white cotton with embroidery—they can all be combined in a hundred different ways to reflect the personality of a child and the family as a whole.

One of the myths of decorating a child's room is that it needs fabrics in bright primary colors and cartoon-character prints in order to be sufficiently kid-appropriate. Children can be just as stimulated and excited by a room dressed in textiles that are subtle and sophisticated. These types of fabrics also have a longer life span. They can be carried forward from the baby years into toddler time and beyond, and they're easier to incorporate into other rooms of the house should you want to move them. When a pretty floral print coverlet's time has come, it can simply be transferred to a guest room; not so a duvet sporting farm animals or ballerinas.

fabrics or furniture: what comes first?

Truth be told, as important as fabrics are to the look of a room, most rooms don't get designed around fabrics. Furniture is generally selected first, followed by the fabrics, which then determine the palette for the walls, rugs, window treatments, and other accessories. Yet there's no law that says you can't work in the opposite direction.

The inspiration for five-year-old Lizzy's room (page 66) came from a vintage bark cloth adorned with clusters of flowers that her mother, Ann, fell for. Team-

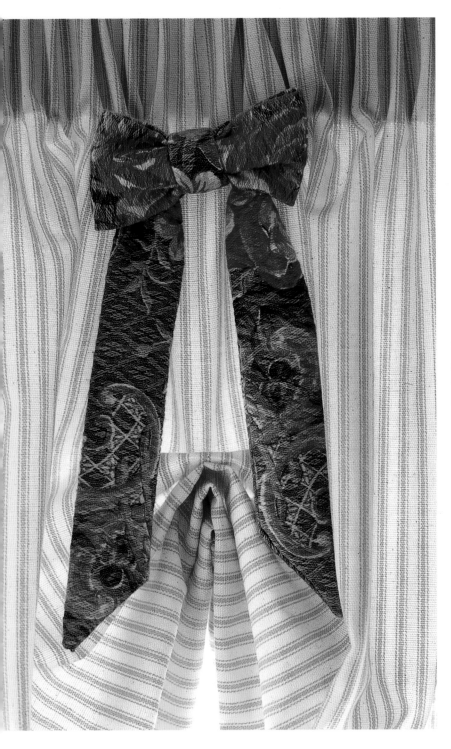

Rather than let some bark cloth scraps go to waste, we turned them into bow accents for window valances.

ing the bark cloth with a green check, we upholstered a child-size club chair, then painted the furniture to match. After the chair was completed there wasn't much of the bark cloth left, but not willing to let an inch go to waste, we picked up the scraps and tied them into bows on the curtain rods.

mixing fabrics

Using more than one or two fabrics in a room can seem daunting at first, but combining patterns is fun and easier than you might suppose. Besides, if everything matches, nothing will draw your attention, and all the work you've done choosing fabrics will have been for naught.

In most of the rooms I do I use five or even more fabrics, often mixing new and vintage. In a girl's room, I might start with a floral, then bring in a plaid, a

solid, a check, or a stripe to be used for bed pillow shams, chair pillows, window treatments, bedding, and upholstery. In a boy's room, I might bring in the same type of fabrics, but instead of florals, start with something like a nostalgic sports, boat, or cowboy pattern or some other kind of novelty print. Or I could pick a theme like Americana and go for fabrics that have stars, stripes, and flag patterns.

The key to mixing disparate patterns is keeping most of the tones the same, but then bringing in one fabric that's bolder than the others to make the whole mix pop. To make things easy, choose one main fabric—one, that is, that you'll be using in greatest quantity (for the bed-cover or to cover a sofa, for instance) or one that you want to highlight—then build around it. Choose additional fabrics that pick up some of the colors in your main fabric and, preferably, have different textures; they add a lot of spark to a mix. A nubby white chenille and a flat gingham, for instance, make good partners, as do a crinkly bark cloth and a swatch of ticking. The only thing I try to stay away from is repeating patterns. If, for instance, I'm starting with a stripe, I won't add another one. Instead I'll look for a plaid or check that I think better complements it.

where the buys are

gently used

- **Flea markets.** At most flea markets, you'll find a few booths devoted exclusively to textiles. I can get lost for hours thumbing my way through stacks of old quilts, lace pillow shams, and printed tablecloths from the forties and fifties. The proprietors of these stalls tend to be fairly knowledgeable about the pedigree (i.e., date and place of origin) of various textiles, but I always let my heart be my guide. If a fabric speaks to me (and passes a few pre-purchase tests; see below), I buy it.

- **Antiques shops.** Many carry vintage fabrics, but you will probably pay a higher price when there's a roof over your dealer's head. The goods, however, may be of higher quality.

- **On-line auction houses.** If you're game to take a bit of a risk, there are plenty of antique textiles to be found on the Web. The photos of bark cloths, chenille bedspreads, and matelassé coverlets are generally pretty telling, although you can't touch, feel, or smell the fabric, a definite handicap. (If possible, contact the seller by e-mail and ask if the piece is from a nonsmoking household.) Still, auction sites are worth checking out since they may also help you find good dealers: Many traders in textiles who use these sites to sell a few wares often have plenty of others in stock that aren't on the Web.

fresh and new

- **Fabric stores.** When you can't find upholstered furniture or bedding that you like, check out the better fabric stores in your area. If you're handy and can sew items yourself, great. If not, look for a seamstress who can turn the fabrics you find into pillows and slipcovers.

- **Department stores.** These days, department stores carry excellent bedding by great designers. Go on looks, but also on feel. Slip your fingers into packages and touch sheets, duvet covers, blankets, and coverlets to see if they are soft but will withstand wear and tear. You may not want to spend the money for sheets with a super-high thread count, but look for ones that are at least 200 count.

- **Outlet stores.** Many designer outlets carry their bedding, usually at a deep discount. Sometimes these items are seconds, but have only minor flaws. Even so, check everything over thoroughly before buying.

Fabric mixes work well on upholstered pieces and pillows, too. A floral pillow with a plaid ruffle is one example; a sofa with striped arms, a patchwork-quilt back, and a plaid skirt is another. You'll never know how well a mélange will work until you start putting swatches together. The breadth of combinations that make sense may surprise you.

Whichever type of fabrics you choose, you'll want to choose them with care —particularly if they're vintage. Here are some tips for buying, using, and caring for textiles.

clever ideas for fabric finds

Fabrics inspire me like nothing else. One of my favorite pastimes is wading through bolts of fabric and barrels of old cloth scraps at textile stores and flea markets. You just never know what treasures you'll unearth—though you need to keep an open mind. Don't, for instance, immediately dismiss a quilt with a few tears or a coverlet with a stain. These pieces can always be cut down and remade into something else wonderful. Plus, you're likely to get damaged goods for a fairly low price.

Fabric scraps are another bargain to look for. Most dealers are trying to get rid of these odds and ends, so they will sell them cheaply. Once you get them home there are plenty of ways to put them to use. The same goes for fabric scraps you already have at home. If you love a fabric you're using for a pillow or slipcover, make sure to save all the leftovers for use at a later date.

It might even be a much, much later date. Years ago, when I was twelve, I was hospitalized with a collapsed lung. To pass the time while I recuperated, my mother and I started a quilt. We never quite finished it, but when

Anytime you use a fabric, save the scraps. You never know what you can use them for later, be it adding them to a patchwork quilt or using them to wrap gifts.

I was pregnant with my son, that never-finished quilt (which, even though it wasn't done, had adorned the end of my bed) inspired me to create cathedral quilt bumpers for Eli's crib. I immediately bought some muslin for the back of the bumpers and put my mom to work! The two of us stitched together old pieces of fabric from the tennis dresses and Barbie clothes my mother had made for me when I was a kid. I plan on saving the bumpers, now a family heirloom, to pass on to my son's children.

when a bedspread isn't a bedspread

One of my best sources for vintage fabric is Susan Felman, a merchant who travels the world to find fabrics. She grabs up everything from antique lace tablecloths to old chenille spreads (her specialty; she stocks about 4,000 of them) and often uses them in unexpected ways. Here are some of her ideas:

- Create slipcovers and duvets from old flags.
- Cut up damaged quilts and frame them like a sampler.
- Swag a vintage tablecloth with a fruit, floral, or travel print across a curtain rod to create a valence. Or use it to make pillows.
- Sew old lace onto pillow borders or glue it on a shelf edge to create a decorative border.
- Use chenille bedspreads as shower curtains (in combination with a plastic liner).
- Hang old quilts from the ceiling or on the wall.
- Turn oversize vintage dishtowels into window treatments by sewing a hem wide enough to slip a curtain rod through.

putting scraps to good use

I believe there's hardly a scrap of fabric too small to be used in some way. One of my favorite pastimes is to sit in my office and go through baskets of scraps to try to think of ways that we can recycle them. Bigger remnants can be used to create patchwork upholstery or slipcovers, duvet covers, and pillow shams, but there are lots of things you can do with smaller scraps. Here are a few suggestions.

gift wrapping Use fabric as a substitute for ribbon. Wrap a gift in either cellophane or colored burlap, then tie the fabric as you would a ribbon.

teething blocks Purchase soft foam blocks and balls at a craft supply or make filling with other fabric scraps. Wash and dry the fabric pieces you'll be using. To make blocks, cut six pieces of fabric ⅜ inch larger than the dimensions of the foam. Stitching by machine (or hand), sew all six pieces together with ¼-inch seams to form a block, leaving one seam unsewn. Trim the sewn seams slightly. Turn the fabric block inside out, then fit the foam block through the opening. Use a whip stitch to close the last seam. Using this same technique, you can also make other shapes, such as balls and triangles.

basket liners Fit a piece of fabric into a basket; trim so that 1½ inches hang over the sides. Fold the edges up by ½ inch and stitch to create a ¼-inch channel for the elastic, leaving 1 inch open at the end. Attach a safety pin to one end of the elastic and run it through the channel. Stitch to anchor, then finish the seam. Secure in the basket, pulling the gathered fabric over the sides of the basket. You can also line baskets by stitching the fabric right onto the basket.

other ideas

- Sew quilt scraps onto aprons to make a pocket.
- Cut remnants into bibs; hem with contrasting binding, leaving long ends for ties.
- Create patchwork blankets.
- Make binding strips or cutouts and glue to a lampshade.
- Stitch together a patchwork teddy bear.

above: Babies love these teething blocks and balls, made from fabric remnants. left: You don't need a pattern to create a patchwork apron. These easy splatter-catchers just take a little cutting and sewing.
opposite: The slightly muted colors of aged fabrics mix and match beautifully. Newer fabrics can be tea-dyed to achieve a similar look.

aging fabrics gracefully (and artificially)

If you like the antiquey look of vintage fabrics but prefer knowing that your bedding and other textiles have belonged to you and no one else, consider aging them with tea. Tickings look especially beautiful with the patina of "age." The process is simple and you can achieve different shades by varying the amount of time the fabrics steep. Here are the easy steps.

1. Start with cloth that has been already washed and dried (without fabric softener). Fill a large pot with water, leaving enough room for the fabric. You'll need approximately 2 cups of water per yard of fabric.

2. Heat the water to a boil, then add 5 bags of regular black tea. Turn off the heat and let the bags steep for 10 minutes. Add a tablespoon of vinegar to the pot. (For large lengths of fabric, fill a bathtub with hot water and add a whole box of Lipton tea that's been steeped in a 2-quart pot of water.)

3. Submerge the fabric in the water and let sit for 5 minutes. Check to see if it has darkened enough, resubmerging if not (keep in mind that the dye will be lighter when it dries). The longer you steep the fabric, the darker the color.

4. Remove the fabric and wring it out. Rinse under cold running water and lay flat to dry.

cleaning up vintage fabrics

Although they are uniquely interesting and beautiful, older fabrics can have a host of problems, from bad smells to stains. If you fall in love with a flawed piece that's not too expensive, take a chance and try these assorted cleaning techniques.

to whiten. It's not a good idea to use bleach on most older fabrics, because it can weaken their fibers (although white-on-white chenille is pretty sturdy, so it may withstand the chemicals). Instead, there are a few courses of action you can take. Try boiling white fabrics in a solution of water and non-chlorine beach for 5 to 10 minutes, then rinse and leave out in the sun to dry (this will not only brighten them, but leave them smelling fresher and cleaner, too). Adding lemon juice to the washer's rinse cycle is another trick you can try. If those solutions fail, try using Mrs. Stewart's Liquid Bluing Agent. Dilute it to the color of the sky and soak fabrics according to package directions.

to eliminate foul smells. If simple washing and drying doesn't work, hang the offensive fabric outside to dry in the sun. Next step: wash with Febreze, an odor remover.

to remove rust. Don't use bleach on rust stains. Instead, use a detergent made specifically for rust removal, such as Wink.

to get out stains. Biz is one of the best products on the market for stain removal. Place the fabric in a bucketful of water with Biz diluted as directed, and soak overnight.

In our factory, we keep bins full of fabric finds, both old and new. Since many of our furnishings are made to order, we often vary the fabrications so that each child's room has a one-of-a-kind feel to it.

acknowledgments

Little Folk Art's *Rooms to Grow In* has evolved over the last twelve years in large part due to a number of wonderful clients (and their children), who not only believed in and trusted me but who continue to inspire me on a daily basis. To all of you around the country who have welcomed me into your homes, thanks for your graciousness and generosity. Likewise, I want to offer thanks for the loving support I've received from a long line of good friends, including:

Alison McCormick, who has been my friend since we were three years old, and who put me together with her sister, Daryn, helping to make my dream of doing a book come true. Many kisses to you!

Meg Freeman, who (even before it became the rage) was always willing to get up before dawn to make it to the Sunday morning flea market. Your talent and ever-so-detailed advice does not go unnoticed or unappreciated.

Jane and David Wyler (and Reusniks, which enabled us to meet), whose basement on Summit Drive housed all of my painted wares and whose backyard lent itself to many outdoor boutiques that brought together lots of family, friends, and neighbors for homemade cookies, friendship, and down-home consumerism.

Eileen Kasofsky, who saw early in the game that I was onto something.

Marianne, who is always enthusiastic about the next thing. Your support and friendship continue to inspire me.

This book was also dependent on the hard work and graciousness of many people, ranging from art directors and assistants to pizza delivery guys. In particular I want to thank the many people who allowed us to come into their homes for the day and mess them up. And a special thanks to all of the children who never complained if we put their toys back in the wrong places. Much gratitude goes to the families of Marianne and Stewart Gilfenbain, Kathy and Lenny Waronker, Debbie and Mort Nathan, Mary and Tony Podell, Deborah and Mark Lindee, Paula and Peter Noah, Gilli and Bobbie Trieman, Ann Hollister and John Thomas, Diane and Lionel Richie, Stacy and Joey Feldman, Carol Kimball and her daughter Erin, Vicki and Jimmy Iovine, Glynis Costin, and Art Streiber.

My staff at LFA has also been indispensable, going above and beyond the call of duty to help with this book. Great thanks to:

Julio and all the employees who have helped Little Folk Art grow and succeed: Mauricio, Amilcar, Gilberto, Roberto, Ruben, Ishmael, Mario, Orlando, Araba . . . and everyone else who has been a part of the LFA family over the years (Suzette, Lori, Tammy, Lisa P., Yoon Hee, Susy, Monica, Hyesoo, Tracy, Joanne—you're all greatly missed).

Susan and Steve for making LFA bicoastal.

Teel, my assistant, right arm, confidant, and friend. Thank you for taking none of this too seriously and for your sense of humor, which always puts everything into perspective. I'm grateful for your ability to juggle so many things at one time and for doing it with a big smile on your face. I trust your judgment, embrace your advice, and respect your creativity. Knowing you are here for me every day makes coming to work so much more fun.

I also want to acknowledge a few others who have helped this book come to fruition:

Romy, for making the absurd and obnoxious seem funny and a not-so-great situation feel fabulous.

Tracy McCandless, for your vision, creativity, perspective, flexibility, companionship, and for knowing exactly what I was thinking. Yet, more important, our newfound friendship.

Susan Kreig, for helping out in a pinch.

Art, for taking beautiful photos.

Daryn, for your beautiful words, your friendship, and for sharing my vision.

Carla Glasser, my agent, for being so supportive and always taking my calls. For walking me through ridiculous situations, making me see the other side of things, and for your belief in this project. Thank you also to Jenny for always finding Carla even when she didn't want to be found.

Everyone at Clarkson Potter, especially Pam Krauss. Thank you for your guidance, especially when I didn't know what in the heck I was doing. I also appreciate the help of Margaret Hathaway, the brilliant design by Jane Treuhaft, and the sharp copyediting skills of Camille Smith.

Great thanks and love as well to my immediate and extended family:

Nancy Grant, for being like a sister to me.

Jeanette, Fred, Tammy, Allan, Sheila, and Marc, for supporting us through all our endeavors.

My parents, Al and Maureen. Thank you for always allowing me to express myself, and for giving me the freedom to make my own choices.

My brother, David, for inspiring me both intellectually and creatively.

Eli. I am so lucky that you picked me to be your mommy. Your gentle soul keeps me balanced. You are my sun, my moon, my rainbow, and my stars. I love you.

Mitchell, my husband, partner, and friend, who gave me the best gift of all, our son Eli. Thank you for supporting me during the hobby stage of LFA, never once complaining when our dining room became a furniture studio. Thank you for always schlepping heavy furniture up several flights of stairs and for putting holes in the roof of your prize 1990 Land Cruiser. Thanks for giving up your career to support mine, which is now ours. Most of all, thanks for putting up with all of the chaos during this project while trying to run our business at the same time. And, lastly, thanks for never complaining about my raging hormones since, in the middle of all of this, I was pregnant with our second child. I love you.

index